1966

STUDIES IN FRENC[H]

Genera[l]

W. G.

Fellow and Tutor of St. John's College, Oxford

University of St. Francis

Currie
Corneille

3 0301 00033972 7

D0123695

W9-ACQ-370

CORNEILLE: POLYEUCTE

by

PETER CURRIE

Assistant Master, Sherborne School

BARRON'S EDUCATIONAL SERIES, INC.
Great Neck, New York

LIBRARY
College of St. Francis
JOLIET, ILL.

© Peter Currie 1960

First published 1960

Printed in the United States of America

842.41
C977

Contents

40137

Introductory

In approaching any play by Corneille one cannot help recalling how frequently English readers have found themselves unable to respond with any enthusiasm to his work. In what follows, while assuming little prior knowledge of anything except the text, I have therefore been concerned less with any formal approach to what is, perhaps, his greatest play, and more with an attempt to deal with some of the difficulties which commonly seem to cause such lack of response; at the same time, I have tried to discuss the remarkable range and dramatic force contained in *Polyeucte*. The very name of the play may mislead us; it is easy to suppose, from the convention of naming a play after its chief character, that it will be mainly concerned with the difficulties with which Polyeucte has to contend in his determination to uphold his Christian faith; even to suspect that, in writing a play about a Christian martyr, Corneille had a deliberate moral purpose in mind. These—or other—*a priori* assumptions about Corneille's intentions and outlook may well influence our reading of the play. I have preferred to remember that Corneille was above all a dramatist, seeking to write plays which would appeal to his contemporary audience. This has led me to discuss the dramatic effects which he has obtained. I have therefore tried to suggest the material of which the play is constructed; the way in which it has been composed; and the reasons which led Corneille to adopt what may at first sight seem a somewhat artificial form. Thereafter, since any dramatist's material can only be effectively presented through the medium of convincing characters, I have sought to discuss the human qualities and weaknesses illustrated by the men and women Corneille has shown caught up in a situation of great dramatic possibilities. In not concentrating at any moment on any one aspect of the play, I have hoped to suggest the many themes and questions which are constantly raised, questions which would have been of lively interest to the theatre-going public of the time and which, it may be felt, have also a universal significance sufficient to justify the study of this play to-day—not as a museum-piece in the history of tragedy, but as an intensely dramatic work which is still relevant to the 20th century.

1. The Background of the Play

Any writer's view of life will be primarily influenced by the circumstances of the society which surrounds him, and his experience of humanity will be gained through what he sees of the way men react to the problems which confront them. It therefore seems appropriate briefly to consider those aspects of the contemporary scene which may have had their part in determining Corneille's interest in the story of Polyeucte, and which may have stimulated him to make use of it in his search for a dramatic subject.

The reign of Louis XIII was characterised by a struggle for power. The nobles, conscious of their feudal traditions and animated, as will be seen, by an all-pervading desire for *gloire*, were trying by all means open to them to hold back the advance of an authoritarian rule of which Richelieu was the most notable exponent. The latter was fully prepared to admit the many qualities possessed by the nobility. If these qualities were used legitimately, in the interests of the State and the monarchy, they could be of great value; but any deviation, any independence of spirit, was a danger and, if need be, must be ruthlessly punished. 'En matière de crime d'État, il faut fermer la porte à la pitié', he wrote in his Testament, and the vital need for the King to show his strength was exemplified by the execution of Montmorency for his challenge to one of Richelieu's edicts.

If overt acts of hostility were liable to severe punishment, there was a perpetual undercurrent of plotting and intrigue. Such intrigues had a variety of objectives, but the energy with which they were pursued was most frequently prompted by a desire to attain purely personal ends. There was little sign among such men of a willingness to admit any self-effacing responsibility to society. Life was constantly risked, not only on the field of battle, where a reckless bravado was sometimes deliberately displayed, but also in domestic affairs, where violence was not only quite commonplace but, often, a risk to be welcomed. In many cases men had retained the medieval ideal that a noble must be seen to be noble by his behaviour, and this led to a disregard of danger and a wholehearted determination to maintain one's honour. Though medieval in origin, the love of *gloire* was not yet out of date; indeed, it had been given a stimulus, even an added respectability, by the Renaissance discovery, through the

8

works of such authors as Plutarch and Seneca, of the old heroic deeds of the Romans. For these men, the right to assert one's own point of view, and to act upon it, could not be questioned. Any attempt to impose a limitation on this right was intolerable, and was seen as a personal affront. It was against this extreme individuality that the developing idea of an absolute monarchy had to contend, a struggle that gave rise, inevitably, to strains and stresses in the whole body politic.

In this situation, and underlying it, the question of the relationship between the State and the individual was of fundamental interest. Without concerning ourselves with the views of contemporary philosophers, it is evident that, for the nobility, submission to authority involved humiliation. As Montesquieu was to write a century later in the *Lettres Persanes*, 'La gloire n'est jamais compagne de la servitude'. But at the same time, there were many in France who longed for a greater stability in life than had been possible in the turmoils of the past. It gradually came to be recognised that the problem of society is the problem of living together. To solve this problem became one of the main preoccupations of the 17th century. Men came to realise that they could solve it only in so far as they could take control of the more extreme (and emotional) points of view which would otherwise motivate their actions. It became essential to appreciate the reality of the truth, 'Quot homines, tot sententiae'; and this required the sanity of compromise if there was to be any peaceful existence. At the time Corneille wrote *Polyeucte* such compromise was still often only a half-felt aspiration, submerged in a mass of conflicting and passionately held opinions; ultimately, it was to find its fulfilment in the ideals of *l'honnête homme* and of *bienséance*. But there was already a growing willingness to recognise the need for authority and discipline, and important sections of the nation were prepared to accept that claims based on the national good were more important than those based on the personal ambitions of the individual.

In the Church, too, there were grave problems. That there was a marked religious revival in France in the 17th century is well known; yet this did not take any simple form. There was perpetual debate not only on various theological problems but on the way in which the Church should fight its battles with the many who had been attracted by the ideals of stoicism and other philosophies. The ideas which had been disseminated by the Renaissance could not be ignored; the problem

of the relative importance of the secular and the spiritual life of man had
to be faced. There were those extreme churchmen who insisted that
religion and the things of the spirit must be the whole of a man's life;
others took a more moderate view, and the Jesuits, in particular, saw
the need to adjust their policies to take account of the profane influences
which were at work in society. But, in spite of this, materialism was a
growing force in the world, and the tension caused between this and the
claims of religion was bound to be acute. Corneille's whole outlook
made him particularly sensitive to this clash of interests. His own desire
for advancement and fame was coupled with the acceptance of spiritual
discipline imposed on him by his Jesuit upbringing. In Vedel's words,
'Son œuvre tragique tout entière est déterminée par le double mouve-
ment d'attraction et de répulsion qu'exerçaient sur son esprit la grandeur
profane, la vitalité païenne. Justement parce qu'il sent la grandeur des
choses de ce monde et croit au néant de cette vie, sa conception fonda-
mentale devient tragique."*

But it was not only with materialism and Renaissance humanism that
the Church had to contend. There were at this time a million Huguenots
in France, who formed a significant element in public life. But to the
Roman Catholic Church, itself becoming progressively more identified
with the State with the advance of Gallicanism, they represented a body
of heretics, whose dogma and view of life constituted a perpetual
threat. For the safety of the authority both of Church and State, it was
imperative that they should be controlled. By 1629 Richelieu had
reduced them from their semi-independent status to that, at best, of a
tolerated sect. Yet the Calvinist zeal was maintained, and their heaven-
regarding religious fervour could not remain unnoticed. And, as always
when religious beliefs are in hot debate, the issues involved spilled over
from the clerical world of the theologians to the secular world of the
ordinary man, a situation which existed not only in France but in England
and throughout western Europe. As Miss C. V. Wedgwood, discussing
Cromwell, observed: 'Strife and fear and persecution was the political
atmosphere of the Europe in which Cromwell lived'—and Corneille was
born only seven years after Cromwell.

Having in our minds this contemporary background from which
* *Deux Classiques Français*, p. 27.

Corneille would have drawn his inspiration, we may more easily summarise the themes which he has blended together in *Polyeucte*.

1. Corneille's generation was coming to realise that a measure of discipline was necessary if society was to have any stability. We have seen how reluctant to exercise self-restraint were those whose prime concern was with their personal *gloire*. To do so would be to deny something of fundamental importance. The whole of Polyeucte's situation illustrates the implications of any such demand for restraint and the difficulties involved in any search for compromise.

2. This need for discipline applied not only to society but to the State as a whole. Could the State tolerate the open expression of minority opinion, especially when there was no assurance that it would not lead to open hostility to the régime? Politically speaking, Polyeucte's behaviour resembles that of men who, for personal motives, were all too ready to seek support for their disapproval of official policy. Félix, confronted by what, to him, is sedition on the part of a highly placed noble, has to decide what his reaction should be; and he is only too well aware that the Emperor will wish to be assured of his political reliability, just as Richelieu was constantly concerned with the reliability of French provincial governors.

3. In a society striving for a measure of balance it was important to discover a proper standard for personal relationships—the desire which characterised the *salons* of the period, and which is reflected in many contemporary novels. This, too, finds expression in the play, in the more intimate problem posed by the situation of Pauline and the two men who love her.

4. The fact that different aspects of these questions appear throughout the play would have been apparent to Corneille's audience. But whatever might be their answers when the issues involved were purely secular, the problems would all take on a heightened quality when, at the heart of all the difficulties, they saw that the claims of the Christian faith were here involved. Do the standards which may be required of a man in the secular sphere become invalid when matters of spiritual conscience are involved? Does an attitude which, as a claim for personal independence that amounts to anarchy, would normally be reprehensible, become, in such circumstances, wholly worthy and admirable? This is the supreme question posed by the play, but, as with all the others, we may feel that

Corneille does not seek to impose an answer, but that, by presenting all aspects of the problem, he leaves his audience to come to their own conclusions.

The task of the dramatist is to reveal, in as clear and balanced a way as possible, the various points of view which may be adopted towards the situation in which his characters are involved. But if the basic outlook of these characters can be said to have been originally observed in the contemporary scene, they are created with such imaginative power that they appear as genuine individuals in the grip of a personal situation; this is far from being stereotyped in development, as it would be if the characters were only 'types', designed as part of an artificial demonstration. Each individual is shown as under pressure from the three main forces we have discerned: the spiritual, the social or political, and the personal; and, just because he is an individual, governed by his own temperament, each will react to the situation in his own way.

2. The Source of the Play

We have mentioned the need for a balanced presentation of the different points of view; a one-sided approach to the subject is unlikely to stimulate a lively interest in its dramatic qualities. Yet the *Vitae Sanctorum* which, in the 16th-century revision by Surius and Mosander, provided Corneille with the story of the play is, inevitably, one-sided. It is solely concerned with martyrdom and, at best, only hints at other aspects of the situation. In the *Abrégé* which Corneille gives of his source, we are told how Polyeucte spat on the royal edict and smashed the idols, 'étonnant tout le monde et son ami même par la chaleur de ce zèle'; how Félix threatened him and sent his wife to plead with him; and how, eventually, he was condemned. At first sight this may seem to give us the story of the play. But in the *Abrégé*, Corneille goes on to list the changes he has made, though without discussing his reasons. If we examine these changes we shall see something of the way his dramatist's insight led him to handle his material, and how he has shifted and enlarged its focus so that we are given much more than a mere account of martyrdom. The picture becomes far more balanced; most of the adjustments serve either to heighten the feeling of tension or to give greater prominence to what we may call the non-religious aspects of the situation.

The fact that Polyeucte embraces Christianity through baptism, rather than by a spontaneous outburst, has several consequences. It not only makes his iconoclasm more plausible; dramatically, in conjunction with Pauline's dream, it creates a far greater sense of foreboding. For 470 lines he is off the stage; meanwhile, a situation is developed in which all the other characters are involved; but while they remain ignorant, the audience is aware of the vital fact of his conversion. Tension is thereby introduced from the outset.

Although Polyeucte's demonstration is fundamentally the same as that recorded by Surius, he does not here attack the idols in procession but during a sacrifice in the temple. By so doing he at once involves both Félix and Sévère; this allows the combination and clash of the personal, the political and the religious elements to make a far more powerful impact. Moreover, we find that Félix, from being simply the agent of the Emperor in carrying out the decree for the persecution of Christians, has become the governor of the province. This further emphasises the political element, since, through being in a more important position, he has greater responsibilities and also more to lose. Thus, the presence of Sévère has a far greater effect on him.

Of those elements which Corneille has invented, the most significant is the wholly new character of Sévère. We shall consider elsewhere his full contribution to the play; but it is evident that he not only complicates and intensifies the situation for Pauline, thereby focusing more of our attention on her, but that he also intensifies the difficulties of Félix, and thus strengthens still further our interest in the political aspect of the situation. Even more important, by introducing a character in the mould of the *honnête homme*, Corneille presents an attitude of mind quite different from that of any of the genuinely historical figures in the play.

Of the other additions, Pauline's dream, besides adding substantially to the atmosphere of expectation, serves to provide an opportunity both for demonstrating the existing relationship between her and Polyeucte, and for her to explain about Sévère before he is introduced onto the stage. The death of Néarque heightens our awareness of violence, and illustrates the reality of the threat to Polyeucte; it also disposes conveniently of a character who would otherwise be a tiresome complication in the later stages of the play.

Lastly, there is the conversion of Pauline and Félix. The precise significance of this will be considered in its proper place. Corneille's own explanation, given nearly twenty years later in the *Examen de Polyeucte*, implies that he was more concerned with the dramatist's practical difficulty of bringing the play to a satisfactory conclusion than with a desire to emphasise the 'victory' of one side over the other. The conversions, he urges, 'servent à remettre le calme dans les esprits de Félix, de Sévère et de Pauline', and enable the author to remove his characters from the stage in a manner satisfying to the audience. Certainly this ending is typical of Corneille's usual dramatic practice, that of showing the calm after the storm. One is perhaps also entitled to guess that, besides more dramatic reasons, he saw in such an ending a possible means of reconciling the Church in its hostility to the secular stage, and of palliating any distress that might be caused by the introduction of religious matters into the theatre.

3. *The Structure of the Play*

The various themes which may be found in *Polyeucte* have already been suggested; but without a real sense of dramatic values, the play could well be little more than a series of speeches asserting various points of view. In fact, Corneille has made his subject extremely dramatic, by constantly shifting the centre of interest. Every scene illuminates some aspect of the complex problem posed when a man's ideals are different from those of the society to which he belongs; when, too, the claims of the Christian faith seem to conflict with those of the world. Yet the play is so constructed that we never lose sight of any of these aspects, while the interaction of the different issues creates a powerful feeling of tension, and a developing impression of that inevitability which is proper to tragedy. In considering the structure of *Polyeucte*, we shall be concerned, for the present, not so much with the portrayal of the characters as with the way in which the author has engaged the interest of the audience in the different aspects of the situation.

ACT I

The opening scene is admirably dramatic, and begins the presentation of the issues which will continue throughout the first act. The conversation between Polyeucte and Néarque poses at once the problem of the Christian facing the question of the relative importance of his family and his God; moreover, the question of persecution, of the relation between the claims of religion and the State, is already hinted at (80–81). Our feelings are at once engaged; we are faced with a question: who is right? with whom do we sympathise? Our own experiences have made us aware of the demands of Christianity, and of our own weaknesses; thus, our interest is directly and vividly aroused. In this scene, the emphasis is on the problem of personal relationships in a context of religious convictions. After being discussed, the problem is then given actuality with the physical presence of Pauline upon the stage; it is seen from a different, feminine, angle. Polyeucte settles his dilemma by a hasty departure which goes against all his feelings for his wife, but which reminds us that the clash between the two emotions which are at work is not something static, but one which leads to action and violence.

These first two scenes arouse our curiosity as to why Pauline should feel so strongly about Polyeucte's intended absence. The explanation is now given—her dream. But first, a new source of interest is provided by her mention of Sévère. Pauline's description of this past episode makes us curious about her present feelings for him; the love interest becomes prominent, with its implications of a triangular relationship, even though, as yet, Sévère is believed to be dead. The full discussion of Sévère and of Pauline's past attitude to him leads naturally to the question of her feelings towards her husband (214–218), a question which, though posed in our minds, is not yet by any means fully answered. After this new element has been sufficiently explored, the dream is recounted. This serves both to justify the earlier discussion of Sévère and to account for Pauline's anxiety.

What we are told of this dream prepares us for the possibility of various new factors: that Sévère is alive; that he is jealous and angry; that he is an important figure in Rome. Polyeucte's death is hinted at, with the suggestion that Christianity is connected both with his death and with Sévère's vengeance. Pauline's father is also involved, and is hostile to

Polyeucte. Over all is an inescapable suggestion of violence, and, at the
end, all the elements of the dream are seen to be focused on Polyeucte's
death.

Thus, in one speech of twenty-five lines, all the developments which
will occur in the play are already suggested to us. The device may be
condemned as melodramatic, and it is indeed true that we have been
given all the ingredients of the traditional melodrama; the dream is none
the less effective in creating a feeling of expectation, and Corneille, with
a sure control of his material, while retaining these ingredients, shifts
the emphasis away from melodrama and uses them to illuminate the
dramatic discussion. However we may view the dream, it enables
Corneille, with the greatest economy, to get things moving and to
create an atmosphere of foreboding. Before the scene is ended, Pauline
has voiced her fears that the Christians may have the power to create a
situation similar to that of the dream, however unreal this may now seem;
this directs our thoughts once more to the connection (which we, the
audience, already know to have been established) between Polyeucte and
Christianity; while Stratonice's final remarks raise the issue of the relation
between Church and State, and also hint at the admiration which the
Christian's acceptance of suffering may arouse. New possibilities in the
situation created by Polyeucte's conversion are thus subtly planted in
our minds, to be developed at a later stage.

We have already learnt that Pauline still has Sévère in mind, and the
full significance of this becomes apparent when, after the *coup de théâtre*
of line 269, the latter's imminent arrival is reported. This immensely
complicates the situation for all concerned; it is also another of the play's
features which are potentially melodramatic. The many improbabilities
connected with Sévère's sudden appearance can easily be detected;
Corneille has indeed been something less than subtle in his method of
introducing Sévère into the situation. But the theatre is more concerned
to entertain than to represent real life; we may well feel, with Voltaire,
that this and the next scene, while frequently offending against probability, are theatrically very effective. In Voltaire's words: 'grande preuve
qu'il ne s'agit pas au théâtre d'avoir raison, mais d'émouvoir'. Albin's
account, besides providing the opportunity to characterise Sévère in advance of his appearance, has an immediate impact. It creates a new situation for both Félix and Pauline, and arouses expectancy in the audience.

Félix fears that Sévère will take vengeance (324); Pauline fears the re-awakening of her former feelings, and twice (345, 349) refuses to see him.

The centre of interest has, for the moment, been completely shifted. Two new problems confront us: that of the nature of Pauline's feelings for Sévère, now she is married, and that created by Félix's fear for his own position and of Sévère's power. Polyeucte's situation is temporarily ignored. By now—except that we do not know Sévère's attitude—all the elements in the situation have been made known to us. Polyeucte has become a Christian, in spite of his love for his wife; reality has been given to Pauline's dream, and his decision goes directly against the policy of the State. As governor, Félix will inevitably be involved. Pauline, with her husband in danger, will soon be confronted by her former lover, whose presence dismays her father even before he has learnt that his son-in-law has rejected his authority. Ultimately, his fears about Sévère will determine his attitude to Polyeucte; it is thus significant that, in the few lines he has so far spoken, the main features of Felix's make-up have been made perfectly clear. With this first act suspense has been admirably created. The possibilities, dramatically, are tremendous. The sympathies of the audience with all the points of view have been fully engaged, and their expectation aroused by a series of unlooked-for developments.

ACT II

The first two scenes of the second act inform us more fully of the precise nature of the relationship between Pauline and Sévère, now that her marriage has separated them. The slight delay before Fabian informs Sévère of the marriage gives the latter the chance to reveal his true feelings for her; but his readiness to submit his own will to hers (372) will ultimately lead him to renounce his love. The atmosphere of expectancy is heightened, since we know that the man who has come between them is now baptised. While we wait for the news of this to reach them, unable to predict exactly what the consequences will be, the interview between Pauline and Sévère holds our interest. Though their language is that of the *salons* or the novels of the 1640s, we can yet share the pain which the situation causes them. Besides being poignant, this scene is dramatically useful, in that it clearly reveals their feelings (see pp. 46, 58) and provides us with a fuller knowledge of their characters. It ends with a moving farewell, which sums up their views of the situation, of each other, and of themselves. Yet the problem is not so finally settled as they suppose; the news of Polyeucte's baptism will profoundly alter the situation.

The discussion in Scene 3 of the still unfulfilled portents of Pauline's dream emphasises the feeling of suspense; this is given further point by Pauline's reminder (578) that there are two problems which beset her, caused by her 'douleur' for Sévère and her 'crainte' for Polyeucte. Yet another factor, not relevant to their recent discussion, is now recalled (592)—Sévère's political power, and the use he may make of any 'irregularities' in government circles.

All these elements have been successively introduced, often with considerable dramatic effect, since last we saw Polyeucte. Now he returns; unlike Pauline, the audience knows that he has meantime been baptised. The centre of interest shifts once again; we are anxious to learn what have been the effects of baptism on Polyeucte himself, and what dangers may develop (now that he is a member of a proscribed sect) from his relationships with the State. This latter question is made the more significant by the position of his father-in-law and the presence of the influential Sévère. The announcement of the sacrifice, in the following scene, makes us conscious that events are moving inexorably forward, and, though we are still not clear how the clash will come about, the atmosphere of foreboding is maintained by Pauline's reference to Sévère's power (632). Coming events are also foreshadowed, even with a touch of dramatic irony, by Polyeucte's promise that he and Sévère will only strive to outdo each other in 'civilités'.

The importance of the last scene of this act in what it reveals of Polyeucte will be discussed elsewhere; but its significance in the dramatic presentation of the subject is at once apparent. In a few lines, the crux of the coming conflict is made clear. It will be fought on the issue already hinted at in earlier scenes: the relationship between religion and society. With Néarque's words, Polyeucte, who in the previous scene had accepted his attendance at an official function as a matter of course, at once accepts the impossibility of bowing the knee to idols whom he has just forsworn. (There seems little justification for the assertion, sometimes made, that he has already laid his plans. Had he done so, knowing that this would lead to certain death, his conversation with Pauline can only be explained as a deliberate deception; but the tone is too convincing, especially as he would know that the occasion for the *civilités* in which he expects to compete with Sévère could scarcely arise. His is an impulsive decision, parallel to that made by the Polyeucte of history.) Now, before he goes forward, it is important, dramatically, that we should know exactly what his feelings are; and, by presenting their different views of the demands made by the Christian faith, Corneille encourages us to make up our minds as to which attitude we ourselves would adopt.

As they set off to smash the idols their fervour is communicated to the audience in a way which raises the tension to a yet sharper pitch. The audience is confronted by a whole range of questions. What will be the consequences—for Polyeucte and Néarque as individuals; for the relationship between Polyeucte and Pauline; for the State in general (since Polyeucte is, after all, of the local nobility) and for Félix as its governor; for Sévère as representative of the Imperial power; and, if only indirectly, for the relations between Sévère and Pauline? The various strands in the situation, to which we have been gradually introduced, are being skilfully woven together; the clash which will involve them all is imminent.

ACT III

The third act opens with Pauline's soliloquy, which does much more than simply reveal her state of mind. Our interest is certainly centred for the moment on her own fears and hopes; for her, the situation is too agonising for it to remain suspended; she longs to be released from it by some definite action on the part of the other characters. But in speculating on the means whereby such release may come, she does, in effect, summarise the present situation, which, for her, is still the problem of the 'rivalry' between Polyeucte and Sévère. Her assessment of their two characters in this connection has overtones of the contemporary interest in the need for self-control to restore stability in private, as well as in public, life. Her continuing ignorance, as opposed to the audience's knowledge, of the grounds on which the struggle will come, and her consequent misplaced expectations, all increase the dramatic tension. Before the end, she turns her thoughts to the political element in the situation. We are reminded that Félix's position could well determine the outcome, since his will be the last word, and his course of action will be decided by his fears.

When Stratonice appears, we know what news she will bring. Here, as
at other points in the play when he wishes especially to mark the tension
(e.g. II. 2, II. 6, III. 3, IV. 3), Corneille makes use of stichomythia so that
the audience may grasp more vividly the horror of what she has to report.
We first hear the orthodox viewpoint of the ordinary person. For
Stratonice, Polyeucte is now an outcast beyond recall (780–784). Then
we are told of Félix's all-important reaction (802–806), which has determined the death of Néarque, but which allows of some hope for Polyeucte, at least until his attitude to Néarque's execution is known. Pauline
recognises that all now rests on her (815–818). If she cannot deflect either
husband or father, all is lost, and we see again how inextricably linked
are the interests of family, state and religion. From this, the narrative
of events in the temple is introduced quite naturally; and this narrative
is of importance because of what we learn of Polyeucte's speech in the
temple. The utterly uncompromising directness of this (e.g. 845–846)
would be profoundly shocking to his hearers, not only because of what
was, to them, its sacrilegious content but, still more, for its political
impropriety. He has asserted that they are in all things completely
mistaken. The new question is therefore posed: should we criticise him
for his outspokenness, or commend him for his courage?

The narrative is conveniently cut short by the arrival of Félix, who
dominates the rest of this act. His fury and potential ruthlessness at once
make it apparent that Pauline's struggle will be hard, if not impossible.
His dilemma, already created by the arrival of Sévère, has become far
more acute now that a wedge has been driven between his family and his
job, and his relations with authority. Pauline's words (906), at what is
exactly the middle of the play, show us with complete clarity what is
from now on the crux of the matter: is it possible for Polyeucte to
recant? But the other characters do not, thereby, diminish in importance.
Pauline's pleading with her father elicits from Félix a series of statements
which, in effect, summarise some of the issues of the play. Intolerance:
Polyeucte is in error (914). Heresy and sedition: the affront to existing
religious convictions and to State policy (916). Politics: Félix has a job,
which he must do (919–920), and the State is of more importance than
the family (926, 930). Voltaire rightly regarded this dialogue ('vif, pressé
naturel, intéressant') as *un chef d'œuvre*. The scene ends with Pauline
making it clear that the ardent determination of the iconoclasts is typical

of the local Christians; from this, Polyeucte's inevitable attitude can be deduced, and our memory of his fervour when last we saw him is stimulated by her reference to their glad acceptance of torture and death. With this scene, not only has Corneille informed us of the present attitude of Pauline and Félix, but he has enabled us to know even more certainly what to expect from Polyeucte. The inevitability of disaster becomes yet more apparent.

With the announcement of Néarque's death, Scene 4 takes the action a stage further and confirms, with specific evidence, Pauline's earlier predictions. By the end of the scene Félix's attitude has hardened; he becomes the determined Imperial official. Though still striving to force Polyeucte to recant, he rejects his daughter's plea. Her attempt to obtain mercy has failed; all that is now open to her is to try to persuade Polyeucte. We are left wondering what success she can hope for, and what will be her husband's attitude in their inevitable interview.

In his description of the death of Néarque, Albin, as Stratonice has done earlier, voices the popular view. What he tells of Polyeucte's reactions increases our knowledge of the latter, with two important consequences. The chance of any change in his demeanour is still less to be expected, and the disaster which will follow this refusal to recant becomes all the more certain. The rest of the scene centres on Félix's own predicament. His various impulses will be discussed later; but, from a dramatic point of view, it is worth remarking that such a detailed and effective presentation of his problem would scarcely be necessary if the play were solely concerned with the martyrdom of Polyeucte. It is the consequences to society, as well as the fact of martydrom, which the play presents. Félix's distress, and the disturbingly human weaknesses which he admits, effectively enable the audience to share in the situation.

By the end of this act, therefore, we find an atmosphere of gathering disaster on all sides. Sévère alone remains something of an enigma. We have been fully introduced to his qualities, but we cannot yet tell what his attitude to the present situation will be. We have not seen him since the incident in the temple.

ACT IV

At the beginning of the fourth act we are at once given a clear indication of Polyeucte's state of mind. As we have been led to expect, he has

no fear of death. Indeed, his interview with Félix is dismissed in five lines
as of little importance. At the outset, he feels that there may be a source
of weakness in his feelings for Pauline, suggesting that the climax of the
struggle must come in their interview. His wish to see Sévère directs our
thought once more to the fact that the part the latter may play in the
situation is still unknown. He has remained in the background since
before the news of Polyeucte's conversion; yet we are never allowed to
forget him. At the same time, Polyeucte's own position becomes more
and more clear. His lyrical stanzas (IV. 2) show that he has, in effect,
already triumphed over the world, the flesh and the devil. Such is his
spiritual exaltation by the end of this scene that we realise that he could
not possibly recant. To do this, even if he were to desire it, would be so
inconsistent as to be intolerable for him. Any agonies which are still in
store for him would be less than those which, for a man of his temperament, would spring from an awareness that his intense zeal had not been
sufficiently long-lasting to overcome the trials of the flesh which he had
deliberately brought upon himself. His decision to smash the idols and
his consequent public proclamation of his faith have taken him to the
point of no return. Thereafter, although there is suffering and distress,
there is no longer any question of choice for Polyeucte. We cannot really
expect him to waver. We shall see the heights to which spiritual fervour
can raise him. Equally, however, we shall see the impact of such a man
on all those, of differing temperament and outlook, to whom the first
three acts have introduced us, and see revealed not only the fanaticism
itself but its ultimate consequences in a community.

There is perhaps no point in the play at which the dramatic intensity
is so marked, or so sustained, as in the interview between Polyeucte and
Pauline. At the outset, Pauline brings forward the most obvious of the
factors which might deter Polyeucte: fear of death, worldly considerations, their married happiness. When he makes it plain that he counts
these as ephemeral and therefore irrelevant, she urges a new argument,
the humanist view (which nevertheless has marked Christian overtones)
of the responsibility which human life conveys (1203). Polyeucte again
indicates that God's demands for self-sacrifice do not allow such considerations to operate. Pauline, realising that his convictions are un-
shakable, urges him (1221) to behave in a way which is in fact no longer
open to him; as we have seen, he has gone beyond the point when he

would be prepared to help the cause of Christianity only by discreet methods. Having declared himself openly, he is fully committed. Any less overt form of belief, still more a public recantation—however ungenuine—would be a compromise which he could not for a moment consider. Offered the easy way out, Polyeucte rejects it utterly. Pauline then turns our attention to the ever-present threat created by Sévère; once he has gone, they can think again. We are reminded that, whatever indulgence might otherwise have been expected of Félix, Sévère's presence makes it unthinkable for him. Sévère's influence on the situation as it is developing is vital—even if it is ultimately determined only by the particular nature of the suspicious politician, Félix. The threads of the material are being drawn ever more closely together.

But for the rest of the scene we are brought back to the purely personal problem of the relations between husband and wife. Pauline at last comes to the question which has been burning within her and which, to her, as a woman, is fundamental; namely, the renunciation of their love which Polyeucte's behaviour implies, and with which problem the play began. This is the one issue Polyeucte has been dreading. Before, he has argued with utter conviction; now, he can only utter a horrified 'Hélas!' For the first time, intense emotional violence and recriminations come to the surface; emotions have indeed been already violently involved, but their operation has hitherto been largely cloaked beneath arguments of a rational appearance. In the latter part of the scene we see the fullness of Corneille's powers in the way that he conveys not just the clash of arguments but also the clash of personalities. We are reminded of some of the outbursts of Racine's heroines in the way the author's psychological awareness enables him to show a woman's reaction when thwarted of something of vital importance. She sees his intransigence as a slight on herself, and gives vent to her hurt pride, her feeling that he has broken his promises, her distress at his apparent lack of remorse, all in a torrent of disillusion. Here is a moment of intense drama. Each has a quite different view of a man's primary obligation. Pauline's concern that Polyeucte should be an ideal husband (1237-1252) is perfectly balanced by the latter's concern to be an ideal Christian who accepts the gospel (cf. Luke xiv. 26). Can the two ideas be reconciled?

Yet Polyeucte is not blind to the suffering he is causing; he can only find relief in the thought (1268) that she, too, may see the light, and this aspiration, now mentioned for the first time, prepares us for the *dénoue-ment*. Pauline resents his suggestion; for her, his beliefs are 'chimères'. For a moment, the contrast between this and Polyeucte's prayer for her enlightenment, his conviction that she will indeed be converted, returns the issue to the wider conflict of pagan against Christian; but quickly Pauline brings it back to the personal level—'m'aimez!' Now the conflict between them reaches its climax; while Polyeucte urges his belief more and more violently, Pauline, equally violent, reiterates her horror at what she feels is his lack of love, at last asserting, with terrible finality, 'tu ne m'aimas jamais!' Polyeucte, in a tone almost of resignation, begs to be left in peace; yet to see her brought to such a violent pitch of emotional disturbance increases his distress and makes the tragedy all the more apparent.

By the end of this scene, any lingering doubts about the possibility of a change in Polyeucte are removed. Disaster can only be avoided if Félix relents; and this cannot occur unless Sévère makes him feel he can do so with honour and without fear of political and personal con-sequences. Otherwise, our main interest will centre more and more on the rest of the group and on their reactions to the crisis created by Polyeucte. The remainder of the act at last allows us to learn what part Sévère still has to play, and what he will be called upon to do. Polyeucte's decision to commit Pauline to the care of his rival completes his renuncia-tion of the world, already made plain in the previous scene, and also serves to turn our attention once more to the relations between Sévère and Pauline.

The last two scenes of this act reflect something of many contemporary novels. In Scene 5, whose qualities moved Voltaire to refer to it as 'une des plus belles scènes qui soient au théâtre', Pauline's charge to Sévère finally answers the problem of their relationship which has been re-opened by the previous scene, and shifts the centre of interest to the question of the 'civilités' (636) of which Sévère is capable. Not only does the last hope of release for Pauline and Polyeucte rest on this; we have here a further example of Corneille's ability to blend the many different issues of the play, for we are at this point concerned with the question of behaviour in frustrated love. Polyeucte's martyrdom is in the background, important only as the occasion for the 'générosité' which Sévère is determined to reveal, and which is contrasted with the view of the situation taken by the 'common man' as represented by Fabian.

We need to reflect on the significance of the fact that Corneille includes, at the end of this act, no less than thirty lines which urge the merits of Christianity as seen by Sévère. Ostensibly, it further reveals his sympathetic character and provides him with another reason for seeking to persuade Félix ('ma compassion': 1446). But it may be questioned whether there is any dramatic necessity for this. Nor are his remarks prompted specifically by Polyeucte. He is talking about his wider experience of the sect, and his feeling that Decius is wrong in choosing to persecute Christians alone. It seems very possible that we have here a subtle plea for greater toleration in the France of Corneille's own time. What he says could, in general terms, be applied to the contemporary dissensions among the Catholics and to the patriotic loyalty of the Huguenots. However this may be, the end of the scene does serve to remind us of the political element in the situation, the problem of what view the State must here take towards subversion and Christianity. This problem is of the greatest importance for Félix, on whom all now depends. Our interest is thus shifted, once again, to Félix's possible reaction to Sévère's request. Will his humanity and his family feeling triumph, or will he refuse to run the risk of political disgrace?

ACT V

Félix's attitude is at once presented when the fifth act begins. We are here concerned with the political factors, and the way in which Félix's judgment is swayed by his suspicion of Sévère. The scene, indeed, creates an effective atmosphere of suspicion and political rivalry, and we see the fear of the man in authority that all are conspiring against him. The scheming and insecurity of the period of Louis XIII are well reflected. A new element is also brought in, the danger from the mob. This has been earlier hinted at (1069-1078); we are shown here that Félix's job is to maintain public order, and if he fails Sévère will have an alternative reason for denouncing him to the Emperor. The governor is throughout this scene concerned solely with politics and self-interest. He makes no mention of the personal aspect, and resists all Albin's references to it, which are those of the ordinary man horrified by facts which the politician regards as secondary.

LIBRARY
40137 College of St. Francis
JOLIET, ILL.

This scene is also necessary as a means of preparing us for the next, so that we may know that Félix's sympathy is a pretence through which he hopes to achieve his political ends. When it fails, Félix turns to his view of what is expedient. For the audience, the result of this discussion is a foregone conclusion. It thus serves less as a scene to carry forward the action than as a revelation of the two men and their effect on each other. Each wants something which is incompatible with the fundamental wishes of the other. It is dramatically helpful that, at this point, such incompatibility should be finally emphasised, so that the inevitability of the outcome is made completely plain. Polyeucte emerges as the fanatical martyr, determined to seek death; Félix as the politician, equally determined to achieve his ends, and exasperated when he fails. This is, moreover, the first time in the play that we have seen them together, and it is important that we should have a clear, and not just a reported, picture of their attitude to each other. Lastly, it is interesting to see that the scene also suggests an element of tragedy which Racine will develop much more fully; here we find the paradox of power, the situation of a man who is able to command everything except the one thing which will bring happiness and release.

The third scene opens with a timely reminder of Pauline's suffering; her happiness depends on a reconciliation between what, as the previous scene has shown us, are two irreconcilables. Her distress leads first Pauline herself, and then her father, to make their final appeals; to each, Polyeucte gives his unequivocal answer. The scene is played solely on the personal level. At the moment of final decision, the political problem fades into the background. And with the failure of these last appeals, the end, which has been sought by Polyeucte and dreaded, in their different ways, both by Pauline and by Félix, can no longer be delayed. The short sharp phrases which conclude the scene vividly reflect the momentum with which the action is hastening towards its end.

With Polyeucte's martyrdom an accomplished fact, it becomes necessary to provide sufficient time for the execution to take place, so that Corneille's chosen *dénouement* can be adequately motivated. To overcome the difficulty, he has devised a scene in which Félix tries, not very successfully, to justify himself to Albin who—as, at one time or another, do all the minor characters in the play—has here again the useful function of giving voice to the ordinary man's reactions. But, though a necessary scene, its positive dramatic value is slight (apart from what it shows us of Félix) until mention of Pauline reminds us that although we know the fate of Polyeucte, we still need to know what has become of her.

Whatever may be its significance in determining the view we take of the play, the *dénouement* provided by the last two scenes is dramatically well contrived to remove from the audience any uncertainty as to the outcome, and to show the effects of Polyeucte's death on those most intimately concerned. Both Pauline and Sévère roundly accuse Félix of a barbarous action, and the latter is brought to admit the emptiness of his worldly anxieties. That, apart from Polyeucte's prayers, there has been nothing said which could, at the time, have prepared us for the conversion of Pauline and Félix, is conveniently accounted for by Sévère when he regards it as a miracle, which of course cannot be explained. (Such an ending would have been particularly acceptable to an audience used to the frequently miraculous endings of earlier 17th-century plays.) All the difficulties are therefore resolved. The new relationship between Pauline and Sévère has already been established. Now, Polyeucte's religious faith seems finally justified; the family is reunited in what Pauline regards as 'bonheur parfait'; and the political problems fade away with Sévère's promise to intercede with the Emperor. For all of them, no questions remain.

Yet for many in the audience there may still be difficulties. What is our reaction to this conclusion? At the end of this play, in which the issues have been so skilfully presented and so delicately balanced, what is the purport of the *dénouement*? Are we really convinced? Such questions seem bound to arise, and on our answer will depend the aesthetic, as well as the moral, satisfaction we derive from the play.

4. *The Ending of the Play*

In the *dénouement* lies one of the greatest obstacles to a satisfactory interpretation of *Polyeucte*. Many have decided that the significance of the ending is the triumph of God over all that has gone before, and they have, as a result, read the play in such a way as to show that everything leads up to this triumph, that Polyeucte himself is inspired by an all-conquering grace. Coupled with such a reading of the *dénouement*, the fact that Corneille was himself a devout Christian has led some to assume that this play was written as, in effect, Christian propaganda, showing how, through the agency of Polyeucte, the power of divine grace is revealed. Yet there seems nothing in the play to enable us to assert thus confidently that Corneille is taking sides; nor can we feel inclined to accept certain remarks in his *Dédicace*—always an unreliable guide to a 17th-century author's true feelings—as necessarily proving a view which, it seems, can ultimately depend only upon an *a priori* assumption of Corneille's intentions. We may prefer to conclude that he has not tried deliberately to influence his audience, but that, as a dramatist, and aided by his powers of human understanding, he has presented the material in a way sufficiently balanced for each of us to make up our own minds.

We have seen how *Polyeucte* contains a variety of themes, all most skilfully woven together and moving forward in a powerfully dramatic way. These themes reflect problems which, in different circumstances and in a less intense degree, were among those which confronted Corneille's own generation. The dramatist's task is to take the questions which have arisen in his own experience and to present them in a way which distils their essentials. But he is equally concerned to write a play which will satisfy his audience. It is not enough to raise questions, however dramatically it may be done; the play must end convincingly. That Corneille has achieved this by showing how God may intervene in human affairs may well seem justifiable; for if, as the play proceeded, we have felt, because of our own experiences of life, sufficient sympathy with the characters for us to realise that each is in an impossible situation, we shall understand that no human agency can restore peace of mind. When men are placed in such a situation, only the grace of God can save them; otherwise, stark tragedy can be the only result. Since it cannot be for us to determine the reasons which lead God to play a direct part in human affairs, we may hesitate to assume that His intervention necessarily implies wholehearted approval of any one course of behaviour. It seems important to bear this in mind if we are not to jump to the doubtful conclusion that, in Corneille's view, Polyeucte is wholly right, that all the other characters are, in the last resort, equally wrong, and that the final divine intervention marks a clear-cut judgment by God on their affairs. Even the most devout would hesitate to regard Polyeucte as an exemplar to be followed by all; yet it has not seldom been implied that this is, ultimately, the theme of the play. It will be argued elsewhere that Polyeucte cannot, in fact, be regarded as motivated solely by the ideals of Christianity. Moreover, his single-minded determination to attain his goal, regardless of the consequences either to himself or to others, is paralleled, in varying spheres of activity, by the lives of many of Corneille's contemporaries. Such men showed, again and again, that it was within the range of human strength to concentrate all one's effort on a single ideal and to shut one's mind to all other considerations. That such behaviour is attributable to divine grace alone can scarcely be claimed as the only possible explanation.

Yet this situation, which has been created by human intransigence, is revealed by the play as one which it is not within human power to overcome. We may well feel, however, that the suffering involved does call for divine mercy; and it is in this context that Polyeucte's prayers to God are made. Only by the intervention of God can happiness be restored; and when this happens, no questioning need, after all, arise in our minds. God has indeed triumphed, as the last lines of the play remind us; but it is the triumph of a merciful God.

Such a view of the *dénouement* can, perhaps, enable us to see the play as essentially dramatic, and not as Corneille's own advocacy of a particular line of conduct. It will also enable us to appreciate how each element in the play takes its full part in building up a situation of great intensity. That Corneille has chosen to end on a note of hope rather than of disaster perhaps reflects his own faith that, in some way, the apparently insoluble problems of the France of his time would one day be overcome.

5. *The Form of the Play*

'La poésie dramatique a pour but le seul plaisir des spectateurs.' This phrase represents Corneille's aim throughout his career. *Polyeucte* was written to provide entertainment, as were all his plays, although academic study may sometimes blind us to this fact. But the merits of Corneille as an entertainer may at first sight be questioned by people in another age and culture, introduced to his work, in all probability, by an examiner rather than by personal choice. In discussing the structure of the play, we have seen how successful Corneille could be in creating suspense and excitement and sensation. Yet to many, there seems an excessive formality which makes the qualities of his work somewhat elusive. We must therefore remember that this play represents the combined effect of three influences; those of tradition, of contemporary taste, and of those pedants who had been arguing for many years about the proper forms of tragedy. All these were moulded together by the genius of Corneille.

Drama, like any other art, has its own idiom, and this idiom will vary widely from age to age. Each dramatist will therefore choose to write in the idiom, or framework, most suited to his particular aspirations and to the tastes of the time. The English, in particular, often find French 17th-century drama difficult because they feel that the authors were confined by a set of conventions which uncomfortably restricted the way in which they wrote. This is to see the famous 'rules' in a quite false light, to regard them as a barrier instead of an asset, even to think of the authors writing their plays in a conscious attempt to prove that the rules could, or should, be obeyed, instead of writing 'from the heart'. This is as much as to say that the footballer who stops play when the ball goes into touch is doing so to demonstrate what a much better game it is when touchlines are employed. In fact, he stops instinctively, not even consciously remembering that it is a 'rule' that he should do so. Admittedly, in the early days of football, before touchlines became clearly marked, there may well have been some exuberant players who preferred not to bother too much about the whereabouts of the line, and others who found their play hampered by the need to remember not to go beyond it; but with time and experience, acceptance of the line became instinctive. So, too, with 17th-century tragedy. By the period of Louis XIV those rules and conventions, which the English are inclined to condemn as unnatural, had—for those authors whose temperaments allowed them to accept this idiom—become second nature. For Corneille's generation, however, there was still an element of uncertainty; for they were innovators, testing theory and practice together until the ideal idiom was found.

A study of *Polyeucte* reveals the extent to which Corneille had emancipated the theatre from the melodrama and *tragi-comédie* which characterised the popular plays of the early decades of the century. Such a tradition could not be thrown off at once, however. Less than ten years before *Polyeucte* was written, extravagant plays, packed with incident, had entertained audiences with a never-ending series of surprises and excitements. Signs are not lacking of melodramatic tendencies persisting in this play. Extremes of attitude and behaviour predominate. The idols are smashed and there are two violent deaths. Of the characters, only Sévère is able to take a measured view of the situation. Their insistence on their own interpretation of *gloire* raises them to heights which would arouse the fervent admiration of the audience. This traditional taste for the astonishing is reflected in the unexpectedness of Sévère's arrival, and in the whole story of his escape; in the consequent complication of personal relationships which his appearance creates; and in the element of magic that persists with the dream and with the conversions at the end—which, dramatically, are only an extension of the literal *Deus ex machina* used in many earlier plays.

Such are the remains of the old traditions; but instead of existing merely for the sake of arousing excitement, these episodes are so devised that they throw light on the essentials of the play, and are all dramatically necessary. By retaining them, Corneille was achieving an appeal not only to 'popular' taste but to the increasingly fashionable *clientèle* of the theatre. Until recently the theatre had been a barely respectable place of entertainment, but conditions were changing rapidly. Many of the audience were now anxious to be stimulated by the dramatic presentation of material which had a close connection with life; no longer could a play's main interest lie in the eventual unravelling of a complex series of incidents. And so, to satisfy the more educated taste of their new patrons, authors were increasingly concerned to provide entertainment in which the melodramatic tendencies would be subordinated to a more intellectual appeal. Henceforward (though never wholly abandoning its earlier forms) the theatre would present 'un plaisir durable de l'esprit, plutôt qu'un amusement passager des yeux'.

The society of this period, under the growing influence of the *salons*, was far more concerned than hitherto with problems of taste. Not only were the *habitués* of the *salons* anxious to develop *la politesse mondaine*; they were equally increasing their interest in the things of the mind.

Words such as *raison* and *bienséance* were applied not only to behaviour but to art. Of art, they demanded especially that it should be true to life; this did not yet, however, imply that extravagance was unacceptable. The novels of the time—as always, the best reflection of contemporary taste—are in fact full of the same extremes and excitements which we have seen were also to be found in the theatre. But at the same time, there was always a reflection of real life, even though this might be idealised.

This taste for extravagance also explains another feature which seems strange to foreign ears. Corneille's contemporaries liked their plays to be something more than a direct representation of life. Actors were expected to strike an attitude, to declaim their lines and, in ways such as these, to portray characters who were all a little larger than life. For this reason, we find the long *tirades* which were popular with both actors and audience, while the play is written in a style which often justifies the epithet *pompeux* which Corneille, with pride, applied to it. This 'high-flown' language appealed to the public, and is sufficiently unworldly to match the striking characters of the protagonists; yet there are constant echoes of the emotions and anxieties of ordinary human beings.

The words of the play have been much admired, and when such a critic as Voltaire speaks of the 'extrême beauté' of *Polyeucte*, he means the style and poetry of expression no less than the sentiments. Many words are nowadays less full of meaning than when Corneille used them; for instance, *ennui* (23), *courage* (170), *charme* (254), *étonné* (361), *déplaisir* (480). There are a number of cases where deliberate stylisation achieves a particular effect, e.g. 571–572; 1281–1282. He forsakes the Alexandrine for stanzas at a dramatic moment (IV. 2). He plays with paradox in a way that has delighted his audiences (1107–1108). He even repeats successful lines from his previous plays (1612, 1671).

The feeling that we are being elevated above the normal plane of existence is also subtly achieved by another of the conventions of the time. In this play we find no action on the stage; no crowd scenes to add 'atmosphere'; seldom, indeed, more than two characters together. The hurly-burly of real life has been left outside the theatre; the situation, and the emotions aroused by it, are here stripped bare of inessentials. Just as the language is refined and dignified, so is the stage presentation. There is no need for emphasis on time and place; all is focused on the main issue, the moral struggle.

But besides his attempts to satisfy the tastes of the theatre-going public, Corneille was also aware of the growing influence of the theorists. Ever since the rediscovery of Aristotle (now regarded by all as the supreme arbiter), there had been many who argued endlessly on the precise implications of the *Poetics*, in their attempts to determine the ideal form of tragedy. The conclusions of these commentators had gradually been distilled so that the broad outlines of such a form were agreed, and we find that the activities of the pedants had led to the same general conclusions as those of the salons. *Vraisemblance*, the search for truth, was the criterion, and it was to support this general principle that most of the other 'rules' can be said to have developed.

That this should lead, among other things, to an acceptance of the apparent restriction imposed by the unities need not surprise us. This was an age which acquiesced in the need for unity and regulation in the spheres not only of literature but of art generally, of government and of behaviour. We find the extravagances of a baroque culture fusing with the greater formalism of classicism, and Corneille can be said to mark the meeting-point of the two in the theatre. The same fundamental causes which led to a growing (if, as yet, unfulfilled) desire for discipline in political and social life were also felt in literature. The fact that Corneille in this play needed to give conscious thought to the unities is evident from the *Examen* he later wrote; but although he devotes some space to a consideration of the difficulties here experienced in observing the unities of place and time, we may feel disposed to agree with him that 'les scrupules qui peuvent naître touchant ces deux dernières se dissiperont aisément'. The unity of action is perhaps more interesting. In examining the structure of the play, we have seen how several superficially different themes are all included; but by the end of the play we find that all of them meet in a focal point, the challenge which Polyeucte has thrown down. Thus we are led to see the truth of Corneille's words in the *Examen d'Horace*: 'l'unité de péril d'un héros dans la tragédie fait l'unité d'action; et quand il en est garanti, la pièce est finie'. The unity of action also required the adequate motivation and preparation of each development; this we have seen to be entirely fulfilled. Everything leads up to the climax; and, the situation once established, no new elements intervene.

It is, however, less the restrictive—and therefore negative—effects of the unities which should concern us than the positive advantages to be derived from their observance. The earlier authors had made no pretence of considering the unities; for them, the complication of the action, with the consequent extension of both time and place, had been an integral part of the entertainment they sought to devise. But the vast increase of concentration provided by the unities was exactly suited to the new type of drama, which was concerned not so much with men's deeds as with their thoughts and emotions. The less distracted the audience were by changes of place or intricacies of plot, the more they could be stimulated by the problems of the characters themselves, and the more they could discern of the human truth of the situation.

Fundamentally, therefore, the unities were an aid to *vraisemblance*. Yet we may well object that the subject of the play is itself far from *vraisemblable*. In what way, we may ask, is such a situation true to life? Corneille himself provides the explanation. At a time when his contemporaries were almost unanimous in their insistence on *vraisemblance* he was bold enough to write: 'Je ne craindrai pas d'avancer que le sujet d'une belle tragédie doit n'être pas vraisemblable.' This was because the *grandeur* proper to tragedy is not to be found in everyday life. Only in extreme circumstances are the essential qualities and weaknesses of human beings revealed. Normally, they are overlaid by convention and a mixture of motives. It is for this reason that he turns to history for his subjects. If an event is authenticated by history, the charge cannot be made that it is impossible. Thus, only in history can subjects be found which are sufficiently striking and which are, at the same time, fundamentally *vraisemblable* in that they reveal the forces which may determine human behaviour. Thus, in the author's search for subjects which are extraordinary and yet 'real', only people of high rank will be involved; for, as he remarks in his *Épitre à M. de Zuylichem*, although those of lesser status may well be involved in similar circumstances, history does not generally bother to record the fact. History, however, may legitimately be adapted if to do so serves the purpose of the author; we have seen how he has done this in *Polyeucte*. Such alterations must nevertheless be made with discretion, lest they transgress what is *vraisemblable* or go against what is common knowledge.

For Corneille, as has been said, the prime aim was to please the public. All rules were subordinate to this; but if moral value were also derived from the play, so much the better. Indeed, the play's concern with truth, or what he called 'la naïve peinture des mœurs', satisfied the desire for both pleasure and edification. That his public did derive instruction as well as enjoyment from his plays is borne out by Mme de Motteville who, writing at this time, observed: 'Corneille ... avait enrichi le théâtre de belles pièces dont la morale pouvait servir de leçon à corriger le dérèglement des passions humaines.' This accords with Corneille's own words on the subjects appropriate to tragedy: 'Les grands sujets qui remuent fortement les passions, et en opposent l'impétuosité aux lois du devoir ou aux tendresses du sang.'

These 'grands sujets' were presented by Corneille with a skill which, when one considers the lack of any serious theatrical tradition before his time, was truly remarkable. Within the framework which he adopted, guided by his sensitive awareness of public taste, he was able to create plays of range and depth; plays which, by what they showed of human nature, provided a stimulus, both aesthetic and intellectual, that achieved the object of entertainment for which he so constantly sought.

Corneille's technical mastery is of course only one side of his achievement. We must never forget that the plays ultimately depend for their success upon the humanity of the characters; and the way in which he shows the 'impétuosité', the 'dérèglement' of men's passions, referred to above, may become evident when we consider the various individuals whom we find in *Polyeucte*.

6. Polyeucte

There have been those who are inclined to see in Corneille's work a representation of the triumph of reason, and to regard the theme of his plays as a conflict between reason and emotion, between love and duty. It is true that his chief characters often claim that they are acting reasonably and are following the path of duty. In this play, Polyeucte has no doubt that it is his duty to throw aside all worldly considerations and all human relationships, and to seek death in order to proclaim his beliefs. He asserts that reason demands it; yet rational reflection has at no stage been evident in his approach to the situation.

That we can admire his self-sacrifice and admit his ardour is not in question. These have, none the less, been provoked by an impulsive act, a sudden unreflecting decision. It was not, rationally speaking, imperative to smash the idols; indeed, various synods of the early Church had been inclined to pronounce against such action. But Polyeucte does not consider the circumstances or the consequences—or even whether it is unquestionably right to act thus. He simply jumps to the conclusion that to espouse Christianity is to accept the call to martyrdom, and in the fervour of his new-found faith he persuades Néarque to follow him. His actions are thus based on an emotional, not a rational, response; we cannot regard him as one of those who, with superhuman lack of feeling, subjugate all else to the claims of reason. Though later he is unresponsive to all appeals, it is not that he is incapable of emotion; but his capacity for deep feeling is revealed in a passionate attachment to one particular course of action, so complete that it dominates all those other emotions which we would expect to influence our own behaviour.

Thus, he accepts his own instinctive responses, rather than rational judgment, as the arbiter of his behaviour. Thereafter, everything he says and does is part of his desire to give free rein to the yearning within him. It is not, as has sometimes been suggested, his will-power which enables him to triumph; rather, it is the driving force of an all-pervading passion, in which we may also discern the effects of divine grace. For at certain moments in the play, Polyeucte's spiritual exaltation is such that he appears fortified by the power of grace working within him. It may, however, be doubted whether, in spite of what has been implied by various writers from Sainte-Beuve onwards, Corneille is in this play primarily concerned with a dramatic representation of the power of grace. The Jesuit–Jansenist controversy had not yet really broken out (the *Augustinus* itself was only published in 1640, and Arnauld's *De la fréquente communion*, which sparked off this argument, appeared in 1643, after the production of *Polyeucte*); and although the general question of grace had aroused considerable discussion in certain quarters over many years, there seems no real reason to suppose that this was a matter of lively interest to the ordinary theatre-going public for whom Corneille was writing, and whose interest he was so anxious to awaken in his attempt to provide them with dramatic entertainment. Yet in his conception of the character of Polyeucte, it seems equally reasonable to suppose that Corneille, educated as he was by the Jesuits, would feel it appropriate to apply the Molinist theory of grace, that a man must co-operate before grace could work effectively. That Polyeucte had an intense desire to serve God is beyond question; thus, for the Jesuits, his ardour would lead to a corresponding inflow of divine grace. In Polyeucte, we see the growing power of both the human and the divine elements; such a conception of the character affords a further explanation for the way Corneille has adjusted the original history to allow of Polyeucte's baptism, since, through his voluntary acceptance of baptism, divine grace could begin to operate.

As his passionate desire to serve God becomes more and more potent, so the power of other emotions to influence him diminishes. When first he speaks in the play, we see him capable of a deep emotion for his wife; but later this human love comes into conflict not only with his love for what is divine but with his passionate desire to sacrifice himself and to demonstrate his beliefs to all. The clash between these passions cannot be resolved by compromise; for him, these are rival emotions representing the claims of two distinct worlds, and he cannot live in both at once. The existence of such a clash first appears to him in the opening scene:

> Pour se donner à lui, faut-il n'aimer personne?
>
> (I. 1: 69)

and

> Je brûle d'en porter la glorieuse marque.
> Mais Pauline s'afflige . . .
>
> (ib.: 94)

Then his impulsive decision to smash the idols commits him to an irrevocable loyalty to his heavenly desires. This does not mean that he is no longer conscious of Pauline's charms; his words in IV. 1 make it plain that he realises that their power to bring him back to earth might even yet prove a fatal weakness. He does not forget, either, that there are responsibilities within the world:

> Je dois ma vie au peuple, au prince, à sa couronne
>
> (IV. 3: 1211)

But we have seen earlier (page 22) that, henceforward, to recant is an impossibility. The claims of this world must therefore be abandoned: all

must be subordinated to his passionate desire for martyrdom. His
soliloquy in IV. 2, lines lyrical in their spiritual intensity, are other-
worldly in tone; he is not submitting his feelings to a logical analysis, but
is giving expression to the emotional forces within him. Here we see his
love of God triumphant, a final awareness that the things of this world
are no longer relevant to his situation.

It is this awareness which gives coherent meaning to lines which might
otherwise seem inhumanly harsh:

> Je ne vous connais plus, si vous n'êtes chrétienne.
>
> (V. 3: 1612)

Pauline is of the world; now that Polyeucte's whole being is pervaded
by his desire to serve God in the way he has chosen, he has turned his
back on the world, and, unless Pauline can take the same step, they
cannot be reunited. It is in this connection that we should consider his
attempt to confide Pauline to Sévère's safe keeping. Here, too, there
seems to be an impulsive gesture; the idea has struck him, and he is
intent on making it his last action before his death. We may feel inclined
to agree with Voltaire that such an action is unnecessary; certainly the
fact that he can make the proposal at all suggests that he lacks a proper
understanding of his wife's feelings. But however much he may, mis-
takenly, suppose that he is thereby doing what he can to provide for her
future happiness, we may also see in it his final gesture of renunciation.
It marks for him the satisfactory conclusion of his remaining earthly
responsibilities, responsibilities which, although the decision had been
taken beforehand, he no doubt feels all the more acutely after the pain
which his discussion with Pauline has caused him.

If we find ourselves in some sympathy with those who object that the
ability Polyeucte shows to cast off the shackles of the world is not that
of the ordinary man, that he is, while recognising the hurt he is doing
to his wife, too harsh and uncompromising, and that he is, in con-
sequence, not sufficiently like ourselves to be a satisfying dramatic
character, we have failed to recognise that he is only unlike us in degree.
The intensity of his emotions is beyond the average man's experience;
but we all have moments when we act on the inspiration of an impulse.
When we do so, responding to something deep within us, we may often
be acting in a way more true to our real selves than if, more reflecting,

more cautious, we take careful account of the other elements in the situation and act—perhaps like Félix—with greater regard for expediency. Having thereby committed ourselves to a course of action, we may often justify it in the name of duty, realising that to draw back would be to deny the truth which lies within us. Such truth may not be easily defined, but it will be deeply felt; we fall back, like Polyeucte, on the assertion that we are right, trusting that the evident sincerity of the action will commend the action itself to others. Thus, Polyeucte urges Pauline to follow him; as justification, there is their love:

> Au nom de cet amour daignez suivre mes pas.
> (IV. 3: 1282)

and the nothingness of life in comparison with heavenly bliss:

> Si vous pouviez comprendre, et le peu qu'est la vie
> Et de quelles douceurs cette mort est suivie!
> (ib.: 1231)

And all he is prepared to say in answer to her question 'Quel Dieu?' is that his God is superior to those of the pagans; he never attempts to do more than proclaim his own joy. In such circumstances, explanations are superfluous, perhaps impossible.

His devotion to his ideal is apparent in everything he says; here is a man prepared to face every trial of flesh and spirit to defend what he believes is right. But Corneille has not limited our interest to the spectacle of self-sacrifice, dramatic though this may be. He has also shown us how easily a man, especially one acting on an emotional impulse, may confuse his own motives. Polyeucte has such tremendous self-confidence that he implies that anyone who thinks differently is utterly wrong. For him, the only way to demonstrate belief is by seeking death. The man who does not do this is cowardly and wanting in faith:

> Qui fuit croit lâchement et n'a qu'une foi morte.
> (II. 6: 669)

Such a wholesale condemnation of others may appal us; but we have seen how intolerance was common enough in Corneille's period, when men's first concern was often to justify their own opinions. We may well find in Polyeucte an extension of the contemporary desire for *gloire*. This

desire (that others should see him as he sincerely believes himself to be)
mingles constantly with his more objective desire to serve God. He
tacitly admits that death is not an obligation; but he sees through it a
means of greater glory both among men and in Heaven:

> Plus elle est volontaire et plus elle mérite.
>
> (II. 6: 658)

Only thus is it possible to show of what stuff he is made, and to prove
to himself, to the world and to God the strength of his belief.

> Allons . . . montrer qui nous sommes.
>
> (II. 6: 646)

Like many of Corneille's contemporaries, Polyeucte sees earthly life
as the expression of individual human ambition:

> Je sais mes avantages,
> Et l'espoir que sur eux forment les grands courages.
>
> (IV. 3: 1184)

Not for them any modern idea of dedicated service to the community;
society will be served if its members see before them men whose way of
life demonstrates, beyond all possible doubt and through their own self-
sacrifice if need be, that their beliefs are right. For such men, steadfast
example was everything. Twice in the first scene Polyeucte is represented
as one of these 'grandes âmes' to whom any 'faiblesse' is anathema (2, 86).
Like them, too, Polyeucte sees that the test of loyalty is a willingness to
die. (In this, he is paralleled by Sévère's supposed end, as reported by
Stratonice (173). Félix, by contrast, is not of the same mould; self-
preservation is his main concern.) Thus, Polyeucte feels he can best
demonstrate his loyalty to God by facing death. Such an attitude is
typical of the men of the time, who saw life as a series of grand gestures
in which life itself was, in fact, of small account.

He justifies his attitude by claiming 'C'est l'attente du Ciel' (647). But
there is a further reason. The service of God will bring a positive reward
—a martyr's crown.

> *Néarque:* Mais dans ce temple enfin la mort est assurée.
> *Polyeucte:* Mais dans le ciel déjà la palme est préparée.
> *Néarque:* Par une sainte vie il faut la mériter.

Polyeucte: Mes crimes, en vivant, me la pourraient ôter.
Pourquoi mettre au hasard ce que la mort assure?

(II. 6: 661-665)

The unconscious unwillingness to distinguish between the glory of God
and the glory of Polyeucte may remind us of those young men of
Corneille's period who, without any military necessity, would deliberately expose themselves to enemy fire to prove their nobility.

This question of motive seems important if we are to decide how far
his behaviour is justifiable. The truths implied in the lines of St. Francis
Xavier's hymn seem relevant here:

My God, I love Thee; not because I hope for Heaven thereby . . .
Not from the hope of gaining aught, not seeking a reward

The extent to which a 'reward' is a motive for his actions, and the extent
to which he is confusing personal ambition with Christian duty, will
determine how far Polyeucte has a parallel among the extremists, in all
walks of life, of Corneille's own time. That there is such a parallel, in
the evident desire for 'grandeur', is further suggested when he claims

J'ai de l'ambition, mais plus noble et plus belle:
Cette grandeur périt, j'en veux une immortelle.

(IV. 3: 1191)

For Polyeucte, any successful attempt to make him modify his attitude
will destroy not only his bliss but his belief in himself. Thus, although the
audience knows that Félix is employing a stratagem when he expresses
a desire for Christian instruction, Polyeucte, by his immediate reaction,
shows that he has no wish even to test Félix's sincerity. He reveals his
horror at the thought that the martyr's crown may be snatched from him
if there is a change of heart in his father-in-law:

Non, non, persécutez,
Et soyez l'instrument de nos félicités.

(V. 2: 1533)

His only desire is for suffering; anything less will represent failure, and a
loss of 'félicité'.

Belief in God and belief in himself have thus become inextricably
interwoven. In the last analysis this means that selflessness and self-
centredness have combined. This reveals Polyeucte as a far more human

figure; he is seen to be, in many ways, just such a man as was often to be found in the reign of Louis XIII, a man passionately determined upon an ideal but not always realising that, in his desire to attain it, he may also be satisfying the desire for his own glory.

There is, however, a further, less self-regarding, thought in his mind. He believes that death will also prove a more certain means of saving those left behind. In Heaven, his prayers will be more readily answered, both for Pauline

> Mais si, dans ce séjour de gloire et de lumière,
> Ce Dieu tout juste et bon peut souffrir ma prière,
> S'il y daigne écouter un conjugal amour,
> Sur votre aveuglement il répandra le jour.
>
> (IV. 3: 1263–1266)

and for Félix

> Et c'est là que bientôt, voyant Dieu face à face,
> Plus aisément pour vous j'obtiendrai cette grâce.
>
> (V. 2: 1555)

A confusion of motive is the common lot of the idealist, if not of the saint. In this character, Corneille has shown us not simply an ideal but a particular individual's interpretation of its demands, an interpretation which will inevitably reflect his own temperament. Polyeucte's temperament is represented as that of a man led, by it, to extremes of judgment and behaviour. In this, we are left in no possible doubt about his sincerity. With this in mind, we can find his doings not only explicable but, essentially, human. There may be those who, cautious and conservative, would question whether his choice, judged objectively, is the right one. But Polyeucte, given his temperament, cannot judge objectively. And before we condemn him, we must ask ourselves whether he could— whether, indeed, he should—act in a way which would, to him, be a denial of his ideal.

The situation of the idealist is one of the supreme problems of the play. It is given precise formulation with Polyeucte's reply to Pauline:

> Que je sois tout ensemble idolâtre et chrétien!
>
> (IV. 3: 1222)

Can the man with complete belief in an ideal ever act in a way which does not bear full witness to that ideal? Does not any seeming willingness to condone standards which fall short of it imply that the ideal itself is only acceptable within certain limits? In practice, we all find that we do not always denounce openly even those things of which we most strongly disapprove, whether in matters of ordinary social behaviour or of fundamental moral principle. Does this, then, indicate a lack of genuine conviction in our belief? For Polyeucte, the answer is 'Yes'; and the play is, among much else, a dramatic examination of the consequences of such an assertion.

To pursue unquestioningly an ideal cannot properly be called a balanced act, for to do so involves a readiness, even a determination, to disregard all other factors in the situation, however worthy they may be. Corneille was writing at a time when such behaviour frequently threatened, to a greater or less degree, the well-being of the State, not only in France but throughout Europe; affairs across the Channel provided many an example. Yet if such extremism may legitimately be questioned in the interests of stability, the problem still remains: how is a man, conscious of the other aspects of the situation, but possessed of wholehearted belief, to act? If he believes that, in the long run, his country can only be morally safeguarded by a general acceptance of his ideas, is he justified in going to any lengths to propagate them, even though his is demonstrably only a minority opinion? Those who had seen the steady rise of patriotism, and who were gradually coming to feel that the interest of the State was all-important, might find such a proposition hard to accept—especially in France, with a recent history full of the bitterness and instability caused by just such activity. The problem is acute, in any context; how much more so when, as here, the claims of the Christian faith are involved. Moreover this was, as we have seen, an age of transition; a generation later, the ideal of l'honnête homme would be firmly established; 'l'honnête homme est celui qui ne se pique de rien', as La Rochefoucauld defined him. Corneille's original audience, vaguely conscious, at the least, of the need for some such ideal, but at the same time ready to admire those around them who were willing to dare all for the sake of principle, would have been well able to appreciate the tragic possibilities of such a difficulty.

Temperamentally, it is impossible for Polyeucte to restrain himself; yet he recognises that, by not doing so, he is causing grave hurt both to

his family and to his country. This is his problem, and he remains
agonisingly aware of it. In the end, all the opposing forces are con-
centrated in an attempt to uphold the claims of human love; to Polyeucte,
these are claims which must be overcome, however great the conflict:

> Faut-il tant de fois vaincre avant que triompher?
>
> (V. 3: 1654)

His passion for truth enables him to overcome all obstacles, howsoever
expressed, and he ends with a ringing assertion of his faith:

> Je n'adore qu'un Dieu, maître de l'univers,
>
> (ib.: 1657)

and with the challenging cry, twice repeated: 'Je suis chrétien.'

Whether his estimate of 'truth' is wholly acceptable, whether the
deliberate search for death is indeed 'la loi des chrétiens', are questions
which the play leaves unanswered; we must each determine this for
ourselves. But he believes he is right, and his willingness to suffer for the
sake of belief is bound to arouse our admiration, especially since it is the
product not of cold-blooded calculation (which could even appal us) but
of emotional idealism. We do not feel that Antigone, believing in the
pre-eminence of the divine law, should have sought to convert others by
peaceful persuasion; her single-handed demonstration was inevitable,
proclaiming as it did that human truth, however necessary it may
normally be to defend it, must bow in the end to divine truth. So for
Polyeucte. The normal standards of judgment, upheld by all the other
characters, must be defied; essential though they are to the ordering of
society, there comes a point at which their jurisdiction ends, a point at
which a man must stand up and proclaim the truth he has perceived.
Here is the moment for fanaticism.

7. *Pauline*

'Voilà la plus honnête femme du monde, et qui n'aime pas du tout son
mari.' Ever since this famous contemporary comment, recorded by
Mme de Sévigné, there have been doubts about the nature of Pauline's
emotional relationship with her husband and with Sévère. Yet on our

answer to this question must depend our judgment of her part in the play. It will lead us either to number ourselves among those who find her too unnatural, or to feel that hers is an effective and essentially human role.

The greatest difficulty seems to arise for those who contend that she cannot be emotionally stirred by both these men. The attempt must then be made to find ingenious, if perhaps not always very convincing, arguments to explain those of her remarks which might appear to suggest the contrary. But it does not seem difficult to imagine a situation in which A and B are deeply attached when, for some reason, marriage becomes impossible—a situation which could arise especially easily when, as in the 17th century, marriages were arranged by the head of the family, and not according to the desires of those most intimately concerned. Once all hope, where B is concerned, is lost, A may well develop, later, considerable affection for C (especially if C bears some of the marks of B's quality); a perfectly happy, if perhaps less passionate, marriage can result. This is not to say that A will forget B; and if ever they meet, their former feelings could well be hard to overcome, however much their situations may have changed. That A will, in such circumstances, be torn by conflicting emotions towards B and C is beyond doubt. Such a demonstration of what is, in effect, Pauline's story seems necessary to dispose of the suggestion that hers is an unnatural predicament.

Although Polyeucte's request for marriage has been approved by her father on political grounds, without her own wishes being consulted, our first introduction to Pauline makes it plain that she has, from the outset, a genuine affection for her husband. Faced with his resolve to carry out his unknown plan, her answer—'It's only a dream, I know; but I love you, and am afraid'—has a ring of completely natural simplicity. However, she is aware that her feelings for Polyeucte are less intense than they had been for Sévère, and her memories of the latter, brought to the forefront of her mind by her dream, reveal that, while she feels the comfortably happy marital affection and respect that she owes to Polyeucte's unquestioned qualities, she can still be deeply stirred at the thought of Sévère; this distinction she characterises by the words 'devoir' and 'inclination' (215, 216). Stratonice none the less confirms the evident strength of her attachment to her husband (219).

This is the situation when the return of Sévère is announced. Distress
has already been caused by her dream, reminding her of the emotional
problems she has had to overcome; now these problems, which she
supposed were of the past, are raised again, and demand an immediate
solution. She sees quite clearly that, married as she now is to Polyeucte,
distress can best be avoided if Sévère, physically speaking, remains the
memory he has hitherto been. But her father insists that she should help
him in his own difficulties, and the meeting which she dreads must take
place. Fortified by her conviction that peace of mind can only be pre-
served if she remains loyal to her marriage and to her standards of self-
respect and filial obedience, the interview, for Pauline, falls into three
parts. Overhearing Sévère's last words to Fabian, she begins, without any
temporising, with a clear assertion of the present situation:

> Oui, je l'aime, seigneur, et n'en fais point d'excuse.
>
> (II. 2: 461)

'What might have been' must be regarded by both of them as irrelevant.
She claims to be moved by considerations of duty and obedience, and to
have control of her love ('sur mes passions ma raison souveraine'), but
this is only part of the truth. Conscious of the ardent feeling which
Sévère still arouses within her, she cannot bear to see him suppose that
she is simply cold, 'résolue' (482), a model of 'fermeté' (485). The
greater part of the scene therefore contains an increasingly frank admis-
sion of her feelings; but she never for long loses sight of the facts in a
situation which it is essential for her to overcome. The scene ends with
her seeking Sévère's help in acting in the only way which can preserve
her 'gloire' (550), her self-respect, her peace of mind. By dismissing him,
she believes she has done all she can to achieve this.

> J'assure mon repos, que troublent ses regards.
>
> (II. 5: 611)

It would indeed be shocking if she were to give way to the feelings
which, as we plainly see, Sévère still arouses. Yet there are those who are
inclined to find her apparent strength unnatural, and to see her as too
virtuous to be convincing. In an age disposed to regard the divorce court
as the simple solution to such situations, this reaction may not be surpris-

ing. A Christian audience, however—and Pauline's view of marriage is essentially Christian:

> Nos destins, par vos mains rendus inséparables . . .
>
> (V. 3: 1627)
>
> Un cœur à l'autre uni jamais ne se retire
>
> (ib.: 1631)

—could see her attitude as not only admirable but essential. Corneille's contemporaries would certainly have found her evaluation of the claims of honour and *gloire* in tune with their own; indeed, the first part of the remark which begins this chapter bears this out. It·is her innate conviction, perhaps more emotional than deliberately rational, of the importance of these virtues which is more powerful even than the emotions aroused by the presence of Sévère.

We do well to remember that, throughout the play, Pauline regards such qualities as paramount. The first words that she speaks (110) reveal how 'honneur' is at the forefront of her mind, and she judges both her own actions and those of others by these standards. She sees herself as 'une femme d'honneur' (165). Conscious of her 'vertu' (167), and determined to remain true to it, she has no doubt of the outcome of her interview with Sévère, however much pain it may cause her. It is this view of herself which supports her when she meets him; indeed, she announces it: 'Pauline a l'âme noble' (463). Whatever her emotion, she must not reveal it (503-504). Where her feelings for Sévère are concerned, whether in the past or the present, she almost invariably speaks of them not only as a torment but as a challenge to her steadfastness, the maintenance of which is a source of evident gratification. This sense of *gloire*, this love of honour, some may to-day find cold comfort; but a 17th-century audience would have been able to share her feeling and understand, as could Sévère, what a powerful motive noble pride could be. This emotional, pride-dominated desire to stand well before the world and before herself is what she calls 'devoir':

> C'est cette vertu même . . .
> Qui triomphe à la fois de vous et de mon cœur;
> Et voyez qu'un devoir moins ferme et moins sincère
> N'aurait pas mérité l'amour du grand Sévère.
>
> (II. 2: 517, 520-522)

To give way to any other emotion is unthinkable; 'ils souilleraient ma gloire' (550). Similarly, her hope that the rivalry between Polyeucte and Sévère will not lead to open conflict depends upon her knowledge that they possess these same qualities. They will surely behave as *honnêtes gens*:

> Leurs âmes à tous deux d'elles-memes maîtresses
> Sont d'un ordre trop haut pour de telles bassesses.
>
> (III. 1: 753)

It is behaviour such as this which she respects, and which she strives to emulate.

That the sight of Sévère has not affected her feelings for Polyeucte is revealed by the fact that, immediately after their interview, she is still deeply conscious of the 'crainte' (578) that she feels for her husband. The dream and the dangers which, as Félix has emphasised, may lie behind the arrival of Sévère combine to create an anxiety which intensifies the problem already caused by the tangle of her emotions. Her awareness of the vital importance of her marriage to her peace of mind (for reasons which we have already seen) makes her realise that she must concentrate all her efforts on preserving Polyeucte (and therefore herself) from any dangers which may threaten in the new situation. But she has no certain confidence that the 'douce tranquillité' (723) for which she longs can be achieved. This is made plain by the many anxieties which assail her in her anguished soliloquy.

But the audience knows, and Pauline is about to learn, that the menace which she fears is as nothing compared to that caused by Polyeucte's demonstration. By his action, her husband has created a situation in which the solution she is seeking becomes infinitely harder to attain. By it, Félix's anxieties and Sévère's opportunities are magnified. When the news is broken, horrified though she is by what he has done, Pauline realises that Polyeucte is still her husband, whom she loves:

> Je chéris sa personne, et je hais son erreur.
>
> (III. 2: 800)

That she sees so quickly what is, for her, the essence of the matter may be felt as a weakness in the way Corneille has drawn her character; but, dramatically, it is necessary not to prolong this moment of discovery, or the balance of the play will be destroyed. For her, although the difficulties are heightened, the objective remains the same: her marriage is the only thing that matters. (It would be utterly *invraisemblable*, because contrary to her character, were she for a moment to see that this deed offers her a means of achieving an honourable union with Sévère.) She must therefore bend all her efforts either to persuade her husband to recant, or her father to relent:

> Il me faut essayer la force de mes pleurs:
> En qualité de femme ou de fille, j'espère
> Qu'ils vaincront un époux ou fléchiront un père.
>
> (III. 2: 816–818)

We know, and become ever more certain as the play proceeds, that the natures of those involved leave her small chance of success. The 'désespoir' of which she speaks (820) is inevitable, and has become so because of the impulsiveness of the man she is determined to save and on whom her chances of happiness depend.

For Pauline, happiness is seen as something dependent on human behaviour and human relations. In her search for it, she is influenced by various factors, which mingle inextricably together. We have already discussed her desire for self-respect, with all that it implies of her view of herself as full of virtue. There is also her pride, and the natural frustration that she experiences when she feels that Polyeucte, by turning to Christianity, has renounced his love for her. (Here we see how, just as Sévère had caused her distress by misinterpreting her feelings towards him, so she causes a like distress to her husband.) Thirdly, there is her sense of the injustice of it all; after all she has been called upon to suffer on account of Sévère, she is now to lose what alone can provide a measure of contentment. And so she can cry to her father

> Ne m'ôtez pas vos dons: ils sont chers à mes yeux,
> Et m'ont assez coûté pour m'être précieux.
>
> (III. 4: 975)

and to Polyeucte

> Quels combats j'ai donnés pour te donner (mon) cœur
>
> (V. 3: 1597)

The man who could set aside all these feelings of doubt and fear is the man whose own action has been the cause of her pain. Dramatic though this is, we have not yet touched the essential paradox and complexity of her situation; for her husband's action, against which she argues so passionately, is also the spark which sets her heart aflame. We have seen her to be a person intensely responsive to qualities of honour and self-sacrifice. Polyeucte's determination to remain true to his actions and beliefs arouses within her an admiration which both strengthens her love for him and conquers her feelings for Sévère, to whom she can at last speak of her love in the past tense ('l'amour que j'eus pour toi'). In addition, the more Polyeucte becomes remote from her, the more she realises—and this is indeed human—what she is losing, and thus she becomes the more determined to save it.

It is this love which at the end brings her release, by raising her above the standards of earthly judgment by which her search for happiness has hitherto been bounded. Her eyes are opened by her love and, with the help of God's mercy, she is enabled, through faith in her husband, to take the step which will reunite them. But though her eyes are opened, her character does not, as some have suggested, undergo an inexplicable change. In the new setting, her outlook remains consistent. As she regarded Sévère's presence as a challenge to her ideals of self-respect and *gloire*, so, as a Christian, she now sees the threat of death as a challenge to her new ideals; as she admired Polyeucte's heroism, so she can now give that admiration practical effect by imitating it; as she longed to be safely joined with her husband on earth, so can that longing now be fulfilled in Heaven; and as she saw her father's fears to be the main cause of Polyeucte's death, so she now sees that these fears can be finally set at rest if he sends her to a death which will fulfil all her aspirations.

Thus we see how her love for Polyeucte is the cause both of her tragedy and her joy; but although the play, for Polyeucte and Pauline, may be said to end in Heaven, we have witnessed an earthly drama. We have seen Pauline realise that the tribulation caused by the reappearance of Sévère can only be overcome by complete loyalty to Polyeucte. Hers is a wholly worthy ideal, the honourable preservation of married happiness. Yet it is the very man on whom this ideal depends who has chosen to make it unattainable. Gradually Pauline moves towards that moment of *reconnaissance* which is the climax of classical tragedy, in which she perceives that nothing can be done to save her, that all her struggles are in vain. However much we may feel that Polyeucte's behaviour is justified from his own point of view, Pauline's presence in the play, and the particular character with which she is invested, serve to emphasise the havoc which is caused by his fanaticism, which tramples upon all normal values. Moreover, it is because of her that Polyeucte's own situation becomes the more ineluctable. Personal considerations dominate in a struggle which would, without her, be the impersonal clash of rival ideologies. Not only is she his wife, the object of a genuine love which he feels himself called upon to overcome. There is also the fact that the love which exists between Pauline and Sévère, and which is the real cause of the latter's presence, is the determining factor in Félix's decision; fearing the combined effects of Sévère's power and supposed jealousy, he cannot dare to treat Polyeucte in the way Pauline desires. Thus, besides the clash between Polyeucte and his wife, we are concerned less with the ideological clash between his faith and the Roman state, and more with the personal clash between Polyeucte and a governor whose view of the situation is decisively coloured by the consequences of his daughter's past misfortunes.

From such an assessment of the part she plays, it can, perhaps, be asserted that modification of any aspect of Pauline's character would have its effect upon the whole situation. The way in which Corneille has drawn her reveals how in this play he has not been content to present different points of view. This he has indeed achieved; but the play is founded upon personalities, and depends for its development upon the particular human qualities of those concerned. Human relationships, rather than points of view, are the decisive elements.

8. Félix

One of the greatest difficulties which is bound to confront us when considering the part of Félix is his conversion at the end of the play. Whereas Polyeucte and Pauline, even though an element of self-centredness can be discerned in their behaviour, can both be regarded as strong characters, defending a principle which seems to them to be all-important, Félix is weak, holding fast to no single ideal, concerned with

nothing so much as self-preservation. If we feel that Corneille is anxious
to show how grace descends on those whose life has merited it, we can
see that Polyeucte and Pauline have, each in their own way, proved
themselves worthy; but we will find it harder to attempt a like explanation for Félix. It has, however, already been suggested that, in designing
this *dénouement*, Corneille was primarily concerned with providing a
satisfactory conclusion to his drama. To achieve this, he felt it appropriate
to show how God's mercy can descend to relieve the sufferings of men.
Félix's conversion thus becomes intelligible, for he has indeed suffered
from the situation caused by Polyeucte's determination to serve God in
the way which he feels is demanded of him. With the awakening which
comes through God's merciful grace and the prayers of Polyeucte,
Félix is brought to see the true nature of the 'cruautés' (1765) which
human weakness has led him to commit in the defence of security.

It is his weakness, indeed, which most readily strikes us, and which
makes us feel that he is, of all the characters, the nearest to our own
experience. At a time when tragic characters were expected to be noble
and heroic, Corneille's introduction of such a man was a bold move; yet
Félix is, dramatically, a highly successful creation just because he is
neither noble nor heroic. We have already seen how he represents a
point of view for which there is much to be said; it is his job to maintain
order, and to give a good account of his governorship to the Imperial
power. He alleges that his job justifies his actions, in an attempt to show
that he is not afraid of personal loss:

> Les dieux et l'empereur sont plus que ma famille.
>
> (III. 4: 930)

But it is not his loyalty, but his fear of authority, which is in reality the
strongest influence:

> J'ai les dieux et Décie ensemble à redouter.
>
> (ib.: 932)

(As at a number of other moments in the play when Félix claims that the
gods are a potent force in his calculations, we may feel that Corneille is
guilty of historical inaccuracy; by allowing it, he has emphasised the
clash between pagan and Christian ideals, but at this stage of Roman
history, 'the gods' were, for an educated Roman, more a convenient
formality than a spiritual force to be reckoned with.)

But besides his attitude to authority, Félix has also a genuine affection for his daughter, and even for Polyeucte. Such affection is disregarded when anxieties press upon him, as when he insists that Pauline should be his mediator with the supposedly wrathful Sévère; it cannot, however, be ignored. The impulses of the father conflict with those of the politician; but he is not strong enough to determine the merits of these rival claims. Fundamentally, he is concerned for his own position, and it is this fear which motivates him, even more than the claims (which he would like to be able to uphold) of his family and of state security. Both these claims are entirely just in themselves, so that we cannot feel him an unworthy character, even though the clash between them, combining with his fear, leaves him weak and vacillating.

His first appearance, with the news of Sévère's return, reveals both the regrets and the fears typical of the man who is unsure of himself: regret for past mistakes, and fear of how a more powerful man may react to them. At once, he shows his self-centredness; Pauline must help him, at whatever cost to herself. Pauline, indeed, knows her father well enough to recognise what will be the main influences upon him:

> Que sert à mon époux d'être dans Mélitène . . .
> Si mon père y commande et craint ce favori,
> Et se repent déjà du choix de mon mari.
>
> (III. 1: 757, 759–760)

Félix's genuine concern for his duty to the State he serves is reflected by his evident Roman sense of justice. But the claims of State and justice cannot extinguish his desire to protect his family:

> Je devais même peine à des crimes semblables;
> Et, mettant différence entre ces deux coupables,
> J'ai trahi la justice à l'amour paternel.
>
> (III. 3: 897–899)

He has temporised, in the hope that Polyeucte, through fear of death, will recant, and so save him from having to make a decision. When this hope fails, he has to face up to the facts, in one of the most poetic scenes of the play. His torment is very real, and very human:

> Je sens l'amour, la haine, et la crainte, et l'espoir.
>
> (III. 5: 1007)

His job, even his life, are at stake:

> Il y va de ma charge, il y va de ma vie.
>
> (ib.: 1018)

At the back of it all is his greatest fear, Sévère:

> Sa haine et son pouvoir font mon plus grand souci.
>
> (ib.: 1032)

Resentment, he feels, is inevitably a dominant emotion in Sévère, the man who, though now the Emperor's favourite, he had once asserted was 'not good enough' for his daughter. This, with the power Sévère wields, will—so Félix thinks—inevitably bring about his downfall unless he can be seen to act with scrupulous correctness. His suffering is intensified when he realises to what depths his thoughts can sink. With his local well-born connections, Polyeucte is a great help in Félix's present position; but his prospects would be far greater if Sévère were his son-in-law. Shame, ambition, fear, these all mingle in the picture we here find of what is, paradoxically, the power of human weakness.

The genuineness of all these emotions makes his an intolerable dilemma. He recognises that, in the distress of his situation,

> Je ne puis que résoudre et ne sais que choisir.
>
> (ib.: 1068)

The father and the politician are made to suffer by the fanatical determination of the would-be martyr. The awful prospects of the coming need for a decision, and the agonising consequences which will follow whatever decision he makes, can only be removed if he can persuade Polyeucte to recant. To succeed in this is thus as vital for Félix's well-being as it is for Pauline. And behind all Félix's anxieties lurks the image of Sévère, awaiting his opportunity. As he approaches the moment when decision can no longer be delayed, Félix reveals the truth of what Pauline asserted to Sévère:

> . . . s'il perd mon époux, c'est à vous qu'il l'immole.
>
> (IV. 5: 1352)

When he speaks with Albin at the beginning of Act V, he reveals all the suspicions and super-subtlety of the political official, and takes a pride in his perspicacity. He sees himself as the skilful man who cannot be tricked into an indiscretion. If Polyeucte is condemned, we see that it will be because this governor cannot believe in the possibility of Sévère acting disinterestedly. Such behaviour is not in the common run of his experience; and because self-interest is at the heart of all Félix's own behaviour he supposes the same to be true of others. He will, indeed, make two further attempts to persuade Polyeucte, partly from despera-tion, partly, perhaps, to convince himself that he has done everything possible; he does, in fact, later claim that this is so, and that he has peace of mind on this score:

> Du moins j'ai satisfait mon esprit affligé:
> Pour amollir son cœur je n'ai rien négligé.
>
> (V. 4: 1693)

But we have seen from his attitude with Albin that it is expediency, more than the claims of his official position, which finally determines him.

Félix believes that he sees all aspects of the situation; but it is his blind-ness to two essential truths which leads him to a decision which causes horror to all except the man he has put to death. If he could have perceived that the 'manie' (1573) of Polyeucte was a devotion to a more worthy ideal than any of those he sought to serve; or if, since that was beyond him, he could have understood that Sévère's 'fourbe' (1447) was a genuine nobility of spirit, then all the distress he chooses to inflict on others could have been avoided. But his pride in his own judgment is a fatal flaw. Ultimately, he even comes to believe that he has triumphed over his weaker self, and manages to conceal from himself the real motive of fear:

> Je me fais violence, Albin, mais je l'ai dû.
>
> (V. 4: 1685)

For the moment, at least, he considers that it is through his own strength that he has reached the end of both his physical and mental perils:

> M'étant fait cet effort, j'ai fait ma sûreté
>
> (ib.: 1689)

and that, in so doing, he has behaved in a manner worthy of a Roman. In this, he resembles the other characters. He sees his troubles as a cha enge to be overcome. But all that has gone before shows that he is here successfully deluding himself (though not Albin) about his motives. We see him justifying, in the name of honour and duty, actions which have been prompted by quite different considerations. We find again a parallel with other characters, the human tendency to assert that duty lies along the course charted by one's emotions; though here the emotions concerned are far baser than those which motivate the others.

Self-deception is at the heart of Félix's personal tragedy—though we may hesitate to regard a man so lacking in nobility as genuinely tragic, however much we may sympathise with his all too human weakness. He supposes that he sees to the heart of the situation; he supposes that he is meting out justice; he supposes that he is defending the only thing which really matters—the security of the state against the unwarranted independence of the individual; he supposes, indeed, that his are the only standards by which the situation should be judged. But, in reality, fear and self-interest are the causes he is most anxious to serve. There are yet other things to which he remains blind until, at the very end, revelation comes to him from without, a revelation which brings with it the agony of remorse as well as the joy of belief. Then he sees those elements in the situation which have throughout the play contradicted his assurance that he alone is able to judge. Others, too, may be motivated in some measure by self-interest; but, ultimately, theirs is a far nobler instinct, for all of them—Polyeucte, Pauline and Sévère—are prepared to sacrifice themselves. Félix, on the other hand, is negative in his self-centredness, seeking the course of action which will cause him least suffering, whether from disgrace or remorse. Such a contrast robs him of any claim to our admiration. Yet his is a vital part in the play. He is the man in power, who has the forces of authority on his side, enabling him to compel obedience or to destroy.

9. Sévère

We have seen how, in their different ways, Polyeucte, Pauline and Félix are all moved to take a certain course of action by some force which, residing within their nature, dominates in the end all other thoughts and emotions. Their situation causes each of them a very real distress; but the course which this dominant emotion leads them to adopt causes, at the same time, suffering to others. Though they are aware of this, it does not deflect them. When we turn to Sévère, we find that—although he, too, is dominated by an emotion, with his desire to justify the constant application to himself of such epithets as 'généreux', 'glorieux', 'honnête'; and although he, too, gladly demonstrates his capacity for self-sacrifice—the part he plays is different from all the others. For his decisions cause distress to no one but himself. He overcomes all normal emotions, but with the deliberate purpose of sparing pain to others. Here we find a hero of any of the contemporary popular novels sprung into life. A modern audience may well find such 'générosité' as he reveals hard to comprehend, if easy to admire. But dramatically he serves a valuable purpose, which will be more readily appreciated if we see how consistently Corneille has presented him as the ideal honnête homme.

Before his appearance on the stage, he has been described in sufficient detail for us to know his qualities. Pauline tells Stratonice that Rome

N'a produit plus grand cœur, ni vu plus honnête homme".
                                              (I. 3: 182)

and Albin's long account of his exploits serves to amplify our idea of him, and emphasises that he has all the virtues associated with honnêteté. We are led to realise that he is unlikely to be the man of vengeance portrayed in the dream, and later feared by Félix. When we do at length meet him, his bearing is all that we expect. To realise that he is not too far removed from life, we need to remember the ideals towards which the cultured society of Louis XIII's time was laboriously striving, those ideals of balanced outlook and self-control which were to satisfy La Rochefoucauld's definition already quoted. Though difficult of attainment, behaviour of this order was not to be found only in the pages of novels. For Corneille's contemporaries, therefore, Sévère would be immensely admirable, but not altogether unreal. We must remember too that refinement of behaviour involves a parallel refinement of language. The seemingly conventional tones of Sévère should not therefore be taken as the expression of anything but a genuine feeling.

He begins, indeed, by referring to his love in précieux rather than

Roman terms; and he proclaims that, if he meets with disappointment at Pauline's hands,

> Je me vaincrais moi-même et ne prétendrais rien.
>
> (II. 1: 384)

Thus we are already prepared for his self-sacrifice; but when he learns of Pauline's marriage, his immediate reaction may seem too pompous, too literary, to be convincing. But whatever our reaction to the manner of its expression, his approach to the situation is made quite clear. Distress is uppermost in his mind; his is 'un malheur sans remède' (421). His conclusion (436), that 'voir, soupirer, mourir' is the only course left open to him, is wholly in keeping not only with his own ideals, but with those often to be met in the 17th century. Indeed, it is a return to the feeling which had earlier led him to leave Rome to seek death in battle when marriage with Pauline had first proved impossible (205).

The same difficulties for a modern audience arise in his interview with Pauline. But in spite of a mode of expression which reveals him as the ideal young man of the *salons*, his feelings are intelligible enough, and leave us in no doubt about his standards of judgment. His admiration for her 'vertu' and her obedience to 'un juste devoir' (526) makes him realise more than ever that the girl he has lost answers all his desires; thus, he can cry to her:

> Faites voir des défauts qui puissent à leur tour
> Affaiblir ma douleur avecque mon amour.
>
> (II. 2: 531)

His distress is very real; but it is the admiration he feels for her, aroused by the virtue of her attachment to *gloire*, which reminds him that these are the standards which must determine his own behaviour. And so, just when his love for her was making him lose his self-control, her reference to 'gloire' recalls to him the ideal of self-respect which is as important for him as for her.

> Est-il rien que sur moi cette gloire n'obtienne?
> Elle me rend les soins que je dois à la mienne.
>
> (ib.: 553)

Such is the figure who will dominate the thoughts of Félix. But whereas Félix sees him as a man to be feared, everything that we have

seen and heard of him makes us aware that he is, in reality, a man whose
greatest pride is in the exercise of self-control, and in his ability 'to see
the other person's point of view'. When, however, we next meet him,
we find that he is not so lacking in other emotions as to be unwilling to
take advantage of the apparent improvement in his situation. One has
the impression that he is so astonished by Polyeucte's action in yielding
Pauline to his care that he is insensitive to the real pain of their predicament. This, besides the love he feels for her, may explain the somewhat
tactless way in which, in a full-flown passage of *préciosité*, he begins an
avowal of the effect Pauline has on him. His love for her is again revealed
as almost the most important element in his make-up; but Pauline inter-
rupts him with an appeal to the ideal that matters even more, that of
gloire:

> Vous êtes généreux; soyez-le jusqu'au bout.
>
> (IV. 5: 1349)

and

> Mais plus l'effort est grand, plus la gloire en est grande.
>
> (ib.: 1356)

A noble pride in his own power to serve this ideal is his most char-
acteristic emotion, and Pauline knows it:

> Souvenez-vous enfin que vous êtes Sévère.
>
> (ib.: 1363)

The blow is cruel; his dearest hopes have been shattered for ever. But
Pauline has found her target; his greatest dismay is to realise

> . . . qu'une femme enfin dans la calamité
> Me fasse des leçons de générosité.
>
> (IV. 6: 1377)

Thus he will seize the opportunity to prove that he is utterly noble.
Fabian's objection that he may be committing political suicide only acts
as a greater spur. He insists that he is not 'quelque âme commune' (1403).

> Je suis encor Sévère, et tout ce grand pouvoir
> Ne peut rien sur ma gloire, et rien sur mon devoir.
> Ici l'honneur m'oblige, et j'y veux satisfaire.
>
> (ib.: 1405-1407)

His attitude is entirely in keeping with those ideals of contemporary behaviour which we have earlier discussed:

> Périssant glorieux, je périrai content.
>
> (ib.: 1410)

For him, peace of mind can only be achieved by the complete subordination of personal desires; the glory to be found in overcoming the obstacles, however great, which fate places in his path is more to be cherished than any lesser emotion. And lastly, his willingness to understand that there is something to be said for all points of view is emphasised by his assessment of the Christian sect (1411–1443). At the end of the play he resolves to use his influence with Decius to secure the toleration which he sees them to deserve.

Such is the character of the man whom Corneille, without the warrant of history, has chosen to include. He provides a direct contrast with the two other male characters, in his ability to take a balanced view of the situation. He is indeed like them in the way he subordinates all his emotions to one supreme desire. But his is not a destructive attitude; when he meets difficulties, he is self-effacing, doing what he can to preserve not merely his own self-respect but the well-being of others. This restraint is perhaps the reason why at the end, although such a worthy figure and although recognising the qualities of Christians, he is the only person not converted. While all the others have an element of impulsiveness in their make-up, he is not the man to give himself body and soul to any cause. He remains the man of calm judgment, unwilling to commit himself. Extremes, in fact, horrify him; the only time in the play when we can have no doubt that he is really moved is when he denounces the extremity of Félix's behaviour. His horror at the execution is all the greater because, if Félix had trusted him, it need not have happened. It is significant to note here that, while Félix is typical of many among the early 17th-century nobility in his refusal to trust anyone but himself, Sévère is represented as a completely trustworthy character. Their relationship reflects the need in France at that time for greater trust: both that people should *be* trustworthy and that others should be prepared to trust them. Only thus could the strains and stresses created by self-interested behaviour be overcome.

Dramatically, the introduction of Sévère is strikingly effective. His appearance in Mélitène is the goad which drives both Pauline and Félix to their decisions. His is thus a positive rôle, for, because of him—even though he remains largely unaware of it—the pressure which is brought to bear upon Polyeucte is greatly increased, and the dramatic force of the situation is made both more comprehensive and more intense. But he is not merely ingeniously convenient; Sévère completes an essential part of the picture Corneille has designed. A modern audience may find a character with no rough edges rather too far removed from their personal experience—though it is interesting to remind ourselves that he was responsible for much of the play's success both in the 17th century, whose audiences found him profoundly moving (witness the Prince de Conti, who wrote: "Y a-t-il personne qui ne soit mille fois plus touché de l'affliction de Sévère lorsqu'il trouve Pauline mariée, que du martyre de Polyeucte?"), and in the 18th century, when people were disposed, like Voltaire, to applaud his philosophical detachment. But it cannot be doubted that, in introducing such a man, Corneille had a definite purpose. As the ideal of worldly virtue, reflecting all that was best in Renaissance stoicism and in the developing standards of contemporary society, he provides a striking contrast to the lack of moral fibre that we find in Félix; but there is also the contrast with the unworldly virtue of Polyeucte.

It was this contrast between Sévère and Polyeucte which perhaps led Corneille to write of the play, in the *Examen*, 'sa représentation a satisfait tout ensemble les dévots et les gens du monde'; for both would have seen their ideals in action. The acuteness of the problem, of the challenge even, posed by the presence of these two men is apparent to-day, as it was to Corneille's own audience. The question is inevitably provoked whether even religious conviction is sufficient justification for violently rejecting the standards of tolerance and self-effacement by which a society (be it the family, the nation or the wider world) can alone be held together. We may feel bound to answer that, in the last resort, Polyeucte is right to reject the world (whatever reservations we may make about his motives). But we are enabled, by the presence of the Roman, to appreciate more fully the tragedy that is involved when the martyr's decision demands the rejection of standards so entirely worthy as are Sévère's. It may perhaps be suggested that, while Polyeucte represents the claims of individual bliss, Sévère represents the conflicting claims of society. Corneille's play may lead us to conclude that the ultimate problem of the world is to find the means of reconciling the virtue of Polyeucte with the virtue of Sévère.

Select Bibliography

In a work of such small compass as the foregoing, many of the problems which are raised by the 17th century in general and by Corneille's work in particular can only be hinted at. There are so many books which can be consulted for further information that I have included here only a list of those which I have found particularly helpful or stimulating, and which are generally available.

Those who wish for more detail on the social and political background can usefully consult

D. Ogg: *Europe in the 17th century*, Black, 1948
J. Lough: *An Introduction to 17th century France*, Longmans, Green, 1954
W. H. Lewis: *The Splendid Century*, Eyre and Spottiswoode, 1953

and, among books published in France, besides the various general histories of the period,

Paul Vaucher: *Étude sur la France de 1598 à 1660*, Les Cours de Sorbonne, 1954, and Paul Bénichou: *Morales du Grand Siècle*, NRF, 1948, may be found especially helpful.

For the theatrical background

H. Carrington Lancaster: *A History of French Dramatic Literature in the 17th century*, Baltimore, Johns Hopkins, 1936

contains much vital information, while there is a very readable chapter on the subject in

G. Reynier: *Le Cid de Corneille*, Mellottée, 1948.

There are two recent detailed studies of the play, whose views of several aspects contrast quite sharply with those which I have here suggested:

J. Calvet: *Polyeucte de Corneille*, Mellottée, 1944
C. Dédéyan: *Les Débuts de la Tragédie Cornélienne et son Apogée d'après Polyeucte*, Les Cours de Sorbonne, 1958

The latter has a particularly detailed bibliography.

Mention should also be made of

O. Nadal: *Le sentiment de l'amour dans l'œuvre de P. Corneille*, NRF, 1948

and of two complementary articles in *French Studies*, that by R. Chauviré, ('Doutes à l'égard de Polyeucte') in January, 1948, and by R. Lebègue ('Remarques sur Polyeucte') in July 1949.

For a stimulating approach to Corneille's work:

V. Vedel: *Deux Classiques Français*, Champion, 1935, and two articles by Professor Tanquerey on 'Le Romanesque dans le Théâtre de Corneille' in *Revue des Cours et Conférences* (Vol. XL).